SOUTHPORT FACES

By

RON ELLIS

This edition first published in Great Britain in 2006 by
Nirvana Books
5 Mayfield Court   Victoria Road
Freshfield   Liverpool   L37 7JL

A catalogue record for this book is available
From the British Library.

10 9 8 7 6 5 4 3 2 1

ISBN 09549427-3-6
(from 2007 changed to 978-0-9549427-3-1)

Printed and bound by
T. Snape Ltd of Preston.

Books by Ron Ellis

THE JOHNNY ACE CRIME SERIES

TITLE	HARDBACK	PAPERBACK	LARGE PRINT	AUDIO BOOK
Ears of the city	Headline 1998	Headline 1998	Magna 1999	Audio 2006
Mean streets	Headline 1998	Headline1999	Magna 2000	Audio 2006
Framed	Headline 1999	Headline2000	Magna 2000	Audio 2001
The singing dead	Headline 2000	Headline2001	Magna 2002	Audio 2003
Grave mistake	Headline 2001	Headline2002	Magna 2005	Audio 2005
Single shot	A & B 2002	Nirvana 2004	Magna 2002	Audio 2003
City of vultures	A & B 2004	Nirvana 2005	Magna 2005	Audio 2005

THE DCI GLASS CRIME SERIES

TITLE	HARDBACK	PAPERBACK	LARGE PRINT	AUDIO BOOK
Murder first Glass	R. Hale 1980	Nirvana 2005	Ulv 1988	Isis 2007
Snort of Kings	—	Nirvana 2005	Ulv 1989	—
Murder on the Internet	Nirvana 2004	Nirvana 2005	Ulv 2001	Isis 2004

HUMOUR

TITLE	HARDBACK	PAPERBACK	LARGE PRINT	AUDIO BOOK
Journal of a Coffin Dodger	—	Nirvana 1989	Ulv 1999	Isis 2004

POEMS

TITLE	HARDBACK	PAPERBACK	LARGE PRINT	AUDIO BOOK
Diary of a Discotheque	—	Nirvana 1978		
Last of the Lake Poets	—	Nirvana 1998		

For further details of Ron Ellis's work, visit his website at http://www.ronellis.co.uk/

Dedicated to...

my great grandchildren whom I shall never know.

Acknowledgements

I should like to thank all the people who graciously allowed me to interview them for this book and and so record their place in the history of our town.

Also, to those who lent me many of the magnificent photographs that appear within these pages.

ABOUT THIS BOOK

A unique social history of Southport in the 20th century told through the words of forty-eight well-known local personalities showing how the town has developed over the years and demonstrating what an amazing diversity of lives its residents lead.

An insight into local politics, business, sport, entertainment, leisure, tourism, agriculture, transport, nursing and the arts.

CONTAINING OVER 150 PREVIOUSLY UNSEEN PHOTOGRAPHS OF THE TOWN AND ITS PEOPLE.

A book that will take its place as an important addition to the histories of the famous Lancashire resort.

ABOUT THE AUTHOR

Ron Ellis is the author of the highly-acclaimed Johnny Ace series of crime novels set on Merseyside and the D.C.I. Glass mysteries. His book, 'Journal of a Coffin Dodger', has been serialised by BBC Radio and was short-listed for the Comedy Book of the Year Award in 2004. He has also published two collections of his poems, one of which won the Sefton Poetry Prize in 1992. He has lectured on Popular Music 1930-80 for Liverpool University and conducted 192 interviews with relatives friends and associates of The Beatles for Albert Goldman's million-selling biography 'The Lives of John Lennon'.

Ron lives with his wife, Sue, in Freshfield. They have two daughters, Karen and Nicola, and a grand-daughter, Emily.

FOREWORD by RON ELLIS

When I began this project in 2004, I wanted to write a book that might be read by people in fifty or a hundred years time and which would offer them a glimpse into what life was like for people living in Southport during the later part of the twentieth century.

Several famous people who live in the town have not been featured in these pages, mainly because, although they might have been born in Southport or reside here, they are not much involved in the affairs of the town. Thus you will find no interviews with Kenny Dalglish, Alan Hansen, Marc Almond etc.

Also, this was why, when I talked to Jean Alexander, I didn't want to know anything about her role as Hilda Ogden in *Coronation Street* but instead asked her about her time spent in repertory in Southport in the Fifties.

Of course, there will be lots of people who are not included who perhaps ought to be in the book. The probable reason they are not is that I do not know about them. Almost everyone that I have interviewed has mentioned new names for me to contact so if you have any suggestions for a possible second volume of 'Southport Faces', do let me know.

I have really enjoyed writing *Southport Faces* over the past two years. The people I interviewed were, without exception, all hospitable and charming and I just hope that you get as much pleasure from reading it.

And if you are reading this in the year 2100, I hope it gives you some idea of the lives we led in our beautiful town in the 'distant past'.

CONTENTS

BOB ABRAM

Bob Abram was born in Southport in 1923. He attended KGV Grammar School from 1934-42 and, after gaining his degree at Manchester University, returned in 1946 to teach Maths, staying until he retired in 1983 by which time the school had become a sixth form college. He is married to Jean and they have one son, Martin, who is a senior lecturer at South Bank University but was once head boy at KGV.

Bob Abram, or 'Fanny' as he was known in the classroom for reasons I never discovered, taught me for one year at KGV back in the 1950's. Sadly, I was one of his less successful pupils. I failed my 'O' level Maths exam four times. The fourth time I took it, I had broken my arm and had to have a master (not Bob, I hasten to add) sitting beside me to write down my answers. If I gave a wrong answer, he would hesitate and cough and I would have the chance to reassess my calculations and come up with a different answer. That was the time I got my lowest marks of all. I never grasped the concepts of logarithms, calculus and pi not to mention algebra, geometry and trigonometry. Being brilliant at arithmetic alone didn't save me.

I interviewed Bob in the conservatory of his home in Preston New Road on a hot summer day in 2005.

When I returned to KGV in 1946, it was strange to call my new colleagues by their Christian names instead of the nicknames that I'd known them by for years as a pupil. So 'Claude' Woodham became Charles and 'Teddy' Edwards was now Joe. Because of the War, most of the younger masters had been called up and these men were working on past retirement age to fill the gap. Some of them were real characters that you wouldn't find in a school today. Even in the early sixties they were wearing the traditional black gown.

I can conform that some of the masters were 'characters'. On my first day at KGV in 1952 at the age of ten, an English teacher called Mr E.O. Shaw informed our class of terrified new boys that 'I don't like little boys and if any one of you upset me I shall squeeze their eyes till they come out of their sockets and roll down their cheeks'. Just the thing you want to hear at your first day at a new school and things didn't get much better.

Our chemistry teacher used to punish misbehaving youths by holding a test tube emitting sulphur dioxide under their noses. If they refused to breathe in the evil-smelling gas, he would rabbit punch them on the back of the neck, causing them to gasp, inhale the sulphur dioxide and fall intoxicated to the floor.

Bob Abram, however, was refreshingly normal and had great success in his teaching.

Maths was a pretty straightforward subject until the early 70's when the education authorities brought in this SMP system in the secondary schools and the rigid categories in which Maths was taught disappeared. There was a similar change taking place at primary school level and I became involved in running courses to help primary school teachers to deal with the upheaval.

Calculators were just coming in when I retired and, of course, now all those things like logarithms and slide rules, which were such an important part of the subject and involved a lot of learning, are things of the past

Bob was also deeply committed to sports activities at the school.

I'd always been involved on the sports side and, by the time I retired, I was coaching games four afternoons a week. In the grammar school days, the only games were rugby and cricket although Hubert Evans managed to get swimming on the curriculum. Soccer was frowned upon; indeed, incredible as it seems now, boys were punished for playing for local football teams in the town.

However, when KGV became a college the choice was widened and students could take up swimming, hockey, sailing (the college had its own dinghy on the Marine Lake), golf, tennis, and even horse riding.

In my time, the headmaster, Geoffrey Dixon, was a keen sports fan and an enthusiastic climber. It was through him that the school bought Long Rigg near Sedbergh in Cumbria where selected pupils went every year to study geography, geology and take part in outdoor pursuits like mountaineering. It was immensely popular.

The 1974 intake was the last admission of grammar school boys. As the sixth form left, we lost the bottom level each year. David Arnold came in 1976 as Head of the new Sixth Form College. Some of the grammar school teachers left, many of them joining feeder schools to the new college. The old building was sinking and had to be demolished but we still carried on teaching in the one block left standing as the new college was being erected around us.

As well as sports at school, Bob has been very active all his life on various fronts on the local sports scene.

Whilst at Manchester, I gained full colours for rugby and represented Northern Universities and U.A.U. I also played in a final county trial match and was a Lancashire reserve for two seasons.

Apart from two seasons at Waterloo, I was a member of Southport Rugby Club and recruited many of our pupils for the team. They would come up through the junior ranks and were the best source of new talent for rugby union clubs all over the country. When the grammar schools were closed, that source dried up and the teams suffered badly because of it.

At cricket, I was a qualified MCC coach and ran courses for potential coaches. I played cricket for Ainsdale Club from 1947 to 1953.

Southport Amateurs Club was started by Joe Edwards in Leyland Road. Joe became deputy head at KGV.

When I gave up rugby, I joined Hesketh Golf Club and became captain in 1991. I ran the Junior section for five years and we were SDGA champions for three of those years. The course is used as a qualifier when the Open comes to Royal Birkdale.

Even at 82, Bob still plays a round of golf two or three times a week. It is obviously doing him good as he looks a good fifteen years younger than his age.

ROY ADAMS

Roy Adams was born in Liverpool in 1932. An ex-Guardsman, high diver and amateur wrestler, he was the last owner of Liverpool's legendary Cavern Club. He opened his first Southport club in 1967 and, since then, he and his three sons have owned several nightclubs and restaurants in the town.

Roy had started his career in nightclubs as a doorman. As a former champion bodybuilder he was ideally built for the job. Not a man to argue with. He quickly graduated to managing and eventually owning his own clubs. His autobiography, 'Hard Nights', paints a full picture of the Liverpool club scene and the gangland culture of the Sixties.

I first met Roy in the early 1960's when he was co-owner with Tommy Barton of The Chequers Club in Seel Street, in the heart of Liverpool clubland. I was at college in Liverpool studying for my Librarianship exams These were the days of Merseybeat and The Beatles and in my spare time, I was running an entertainment agency and managing local beat groups. Every night, when the other students were swotting in the Picton Library, I was touring the city's nightclubs touting for bookings.

Roy was one of the first people to book groups from me in my early days as an agent and I continued supplying acts for his other clubs for many years afterwards.

Now, in 2006, I interviewed Roy in his impressive Aughton home in the company of the largest Alsatian I have seen and in a room that failed to be dominated by the suit of armour in the corner.

It was in 1967 that Roy started to extend his operations towards Southport.

Tommy Barton and I took on the old Beach Club on Ainsdale Promenade in 1966. There was living accommodation above it but it had all become derelict. We renovated the whole building and opened up in 1967 as a Tudor-style country club. We called it Toad Hall because of the Natterjack Toads that lived in the surrounding sandhills. My family and I lived in the flat above. The Lido down the road had closed but The Sands across from us had a bar and casino.

Monday night was the big night at Toad when we put on a free buffet. People came from all over Lancashire. At first, we couldn't get a gaming licence as Southport was not in an area designated for gambling. However, John James at the Kingsway had this overturned on appeal so we were able to open a casino at Toad Hall as we were in the same area. Unfortunately, not long afterwards, the Government legalised gaming which, because of the new rules, had a disastrous effect of reducing the number of casinos in the country from 4000 to 100 almost overnight. By this time, we had a regular clientele of gamblers but now we had to create a separate entrance for them apart from the club. We built a door leading off the beach side but the punters did not like having to face the gales blowing in from the sea on winters' nights and business fell away so we closed it down and reverted to being just a nightclub.

The police created a lot of problems for us. Although nobody but our patrons would be parking along a deserted road beside the beach in the early hours of the morning, they started issuing parking tickets to all the cars. By 1970, I'd had enough and I sold my share of the club to Tony Stannard. Tommy Barton still owns Toad Hall today along with The Sands across the road but, although he still uses the upper floor as offices, the club itself has been shut to the public for some years.

After Toad Hall, I bought Shorrocks Hill in Formby from Eric Armitage the butcher. It had originally been Sir Richard Formby's home. I had Shorrocks for eleven years. The big feature was a giant elephants head that weighed half a ton and came from Eden Hall in Cheshire.

We were big in catering and every Wednesday night we organised 'Around the World Gastronomique Tours' featuring food from different countries. Our chef, Ronnie Malpas, was one of only two English chefs who could spit roast an ox. In the summer we had barbecues round the outdoor swimming pool. I sold Shorrocks in 1981, again to Tony Stannard.

My next purchase, with my sons Rowland and Tony, was Southport's Kingsway Club in 1985, which in the sixties and seventies under John James, had acquired a reputation both as one of the North West's leading cabaret venues with stars like Tom Jones and Engelbert Humperdinck appearing there. But it was also as a haven for gangsters. Mad' Frankie Fraser was running a big slot machine operation in Southport at the time and he, the Richardsons and the Krays, were regular visitors to the club.

I knew the Kingsway in the sixties only too well from my agency days. Ronnie Appleby was the manager and Mark Peters the compére when my groups like The Beechwoods, Steve Day & The Kinsmen and The Pattern People played there regularly.

By the time Roy took over, those days were long gone.

John James sold up years ago, to the Karinis, but the theatre club boom of the seventies was over and the place had been empty for three years. We completely renovated it and opened up again as a high-class venue with a restaurant, top variety acts and a disco. Lovelace Watkins was the most popular artiste we put on but my favourite was an acrobatic comedian/singer called Brian Pierce. Tony Christie was the last name act to appear.

We had a lot of characters who were regular customers. Sydney Cain, a local con man who'd been in prison with the Krays but was a charming old fellow, came in and sang at the mike every Thursday night. He was 84 when he died.

I had good occasion to remember Roy's time at the Kingsway. In 1989, P.J. Proby recorded two songs I had written and we decided to launch his new C.D. with a live performance at the Kingsway. In the 1960's, Proby had been the most popular male singer in Britain but after splitting his trousers at the Croydon Empire his career had nose-dived and by 1989 he was in the middle of his well-publicised heavy drinking period. He rang me from the Dukes Folly Hotel in Duke Street half an hour before he was due onstage, refusing to go to the venue. Roy went across to have a 'quiet word' with him and Proby soon changed his mind. Disappointed punters who witnessed his 'act' on the night might have wished Roy had left him where he was.

Interestingly, Proby never touched a drop of alcohol after a heart scare in 1992 and in May 2006 completed a triumphant nationwide Solid Silver Sixties Show tour climaxing in a standing ovation at the London Palladium.

In 1994, Roy decided to build an extension to the Kingsway.

We dug down 15 feet to put in the new foundations for the extension and eventually opened up as a select restaurant called La Corniche. I brought Gaudi designed chairs over from France to complement the Art Nouveau décor and I painted all the artwork myself.

We sold the Kingsway in 1996 to a national entertainment company called Northern Leisure who sadly ripped most of our valuable fittings out and turned the place into a teenage discotheque under the name of Astoria. It later became Bliss when it was bought by local entrepreneur John Ball. It's closed down now and there are plans to demolish the building and build yet another apartment block in its place.

Roy has surprising interests for a club owner. He is an artist of no mean merit and he has always been a keen horse rider.

The riding gene must have been passed on as my daughter, Diane, was a winner of the prestigious International Dressage Grand Prix at the Royal Windsor Horse Show and I am a longtime member of the Holcombe Hunt.

Unfortunately, in 1997 I was thrown from my horse and suffered a severe spinal injury. My neck was broken but luckily my spinal cord was intact but it forced me to relinquish the saddle and I was laid up for a long while after several operations..

After this accident, Roy decided to retire and leave the business activities to his sons and they have continued to be active on the local entertainment scene.

Rowland and Tony bought the old West End Club in Waverley Street, which was later taken over by Paul and their mother, Ellen, who renamed it EPA but have since rented it out and it still operates as a nightclub.

Paul also bought Broadbents' derelict furniture storerooms in West Street and transformed the building into The Warehouse Brasserie, which has since become one of the town's most popular eating venues and a good place for celebrity spotting.

In the eighties, Rowland worked as a minder to chart-topping Liverpool band, 'Frankie Goes to Hollywood', on their world tours but he returned to Southport and in 2004 bought the old motor taxation office in Post Office Avenue which he opened it as a trendy restaurant called The Latin Lounge.

In 2005, Paul acquired the old Palace Cinema on Lord Street, a listed Grade II Heritage Building and the second oldest cinema in the North. At the time of writing, he has demolished the crumbling Art Deco edifice, with the full approval of conservationists, and is currently replacing it with a luxury boutique hotel to be called Vincent.

Tony, back from a sojourn on the Costa del Sol, has taken over what had originally been the Ship Inn in Cable Street but was more recently a gay bar called the Amsterdam. Tony reopened it in 2005 as a pub under a new name, The Ship's Anchor. Needless to say, it boasts regular live music nights.

Roy's health has not been too good since his accident but, at 74, he still cuts a striking and elegant figure, so obviously those early years in the gym have stood him in good stead.

JEAN ALEXANDER

Actress Jean Alexander is best known for her role as Hilda Ogden in *Coronation Street* which spanned 23 years. However, in the 1950's, Jean came to Southport as a member of the old Southport Repertory Company and she still lives in the town today.

I first interviewed Jean in the late 1990's for my *Southport Nostalgia* radio programme on Dune FM, and when I arrived at her neat semi-detached house in Churchtown a decade later, nothing much had changed. She first moved here with her mother in 1970. Her mother died in 1980 and Jean has stayed on alone ever since. Her brother lives with his wife in Ambleside.

I felt we had something in common as like Jean, I too have appeared in Coronation Street on numerous occasions but, unfortunately, only in minor roles. After I had been going there for several months, I asked about the chances of me being given a speaking part.

'I'm always "man in street" or "man in bar",' I complained.

'Don't worry, dear boy, ' said the Granada executive. 'In the fullness of time you shall become "old man in street", "old man in bar". Sadly, he was right.

Jean's cut glass accent bears little resemblance to either the Northern vowels of Hilda or to her origins as a Scouser.

'I was born and brought up in Liverpool and when I was a little girl my brother and I would be taken on the train to the Southport for a day the Sea Bathing Lake.. It was always packed in summer. They should have put a dome over it and kept it going all the year round. It would look a lot better than the sheds they've put up.

We'd go to Woodhead's Café on Lord Street and my mother would order a pot of tea and three chocolate éclairs and we'd watch ladies in hats chatting away.

The first thing you saw when you came out of the station was the Eulah Butter Cream Shop where you could see the sweets being made on a machine in the window. It was 3d for a paper bag or a shilling for a cardboard box. My mother would always buy us a bag each because if we got a box, my brother would whisk them into his face before I could move.

Then there was the herbalist on the corner of London Street and Wright Street where you could get sarsaparilla, dandelion and burdock and hot Vimto for 2d a glass. I remember a cherry tree that was the first to flower every year. It was on Lord Street on the pavement outside Cannell's. It's gone now.'

On leaving school, Jean worked for five years in Liverpool Libraries. (*'Mainly to read the books and plays'*). Remembering my own years as a librarian, we spent some time discussing cataloguing and classification but Jean insisted that the theatre was always her abiding obsession. In 1948, she left the library and joined a fit-up (touring) company based in Macclesfield. After a couple of years on the road, she went to Oldham Rep but hated it and stayed only four months.

She came to Southport in 1951 for a 'special week' trial for the role of the mad maid in 'See How They Run' at the Southport Repertory Company under producer/director Donald Bodley, and stayed until 1958 when she moved to repertory in York.

At first she lodged at a house in Welbeck Road, where she paid thirty shillings a week for her own bedroom, sharing a kitchen and bathroom, but in 1955 her parents sold up in Liverpool and bought a house at 97 Sefton Street. Jean moved in with them.

'The house cost £1600 and I was able to get a £400 mortgage on the strength of my job as an actress.

When I first arrived at Southport, we played at the Little Theatre. The Sheffield Rep, with people like Cyril Luckham, had been based there during the War to escape the bombs. When they moved back to Sheffield, Donald took over the company and renamed it Southport Repertory Company. It was a narrow stage and the set went right to the back of the building.

We rented it in the summer when the amateurs didn't want it then we moved in the winter to the Casino at the front of the Pier where the Funland amusement arcade is today.

The dressing rooms in the Casino were on the upper floor and the floorboards were bent and hollowed out. Between two of the dressing rooms, when it rained you had to hoist your skirts up to avoid the puddles. The outside walls were tongue and groove boarding and there was a gap by where I used to sit. On a clear night, I could see Blackpool Tower as I put my make up on with the wind whistling in my eyes and, if it rained, your clothes got wet. The stage door opened outwards facing the sea and when there were gales, you couldn't open it and we all had to go in through the front, half an hour before the performance commenced. Then there were the rats. If you didn't put your greasepaint in a tin, the rats would eat it during the night. Sometimes, they ventured into the orchestra stalls and frightened the odd person when they nipped their toes.

When the tabs were down at night they'd eat the gold fringes of the curtains.

Southport had always supported amateur theatre over professional companies. The SDC put on five plays and a panto every year. We had to struggle for audiences in the winter. It was bitterly cold. We used always to wear gloves and we kept a hot water bottle backstage. Anyone waiting in the wings to go on would hug it, ready to hand it over to someone coming off, if the people in the cast outnumbered the audience, the performance would be cancelled and they'd get their money back. Luckily, there weren't too many large casts except in pantomime.

Sometimes we'd walk to the end of the Pier for half a pint of beer at the pub. It was all we could afford.'

When we were at the Little Theatre, there was a dance band playing on the Bandstand outside the Town Hall on a Saturday night in the summer. All around the bandstand there were black and white tiles like terraces. For the last hour, from eleven o'clock to midnight, they'd let you in for half price, I think it was a shilling, to go and have a dance. Norman Cunningham from the Sheila Elliott-Clarke School of Dancing in Liverpool, took me and taught me ballroom dancing.'

The Casino, built in 1902 as the Pier Pavilion, was an opulent building, which boasted 1500 seats and could accommodate another 500 patrons standing. Over the years, it had housed plays and shows and shown silent films but by 1951 it had become ramshackle and, in 1953, the company moved along the Promenade to take up residence in the Scala Cinema which had recently stopped showing films.

The Scala had started life in the 1870's as The Pavilion concert hall, part of the impressive Winter Gardens complex. In 1905 it was rebuilt as the Albert Hall Palace of Varieties with 1200 seats and offered variety shows and films on the Bioscope. It became the Empire in 1910 and was refurbished three years later as the Empire Picture Theatre. Below it was the Empire Roller Rink. In 1921, impresario Alfred Levy opened it as the Scala and it became the first cinema in Southport to show talking pictures when Al Jolson in 'The Singing Fool' was the attraction in April 1929.

After several changes of ownership and management during which time the building was used as a theatre, cinema and for Sunday afternoon concerts, the Southport Repertory Company moved in. Their new venue was warmer and more comfortable than the draughty old Casino and they enjoyed bigger crowds but backstage was as just as grubby.

The dressing rooms were in the basement. We painted the walls white after we'd cleaned away the dirt and the cobwebs.

On a Monday, we worked from 10am until 11pm. We had a dress rehearsal all day, with time only for a sandwich at lunchtime, then the performance at night with a matinee on a Saturday. From Tuesday to Saturday, we learned our parts for the following week's play from 10am to 2am. You had to know Act One by Wednesday, Act Two by Thursday and Act Three by Friday.

When I first went to the Scala, they had a tea interval on a Wednesday and the audience were allowed to take cups of tea back to their seats. You couldn't hear your lines for the tinkling of cups at the start of the second act.

And some people thought we were amateurs! They asked us what we did in real life as if we went there and made it up every night.

In the afternoons in the summer, I'd go into Botanic Gardens afterwards to practice my lines and sort out my costume. Sometimes I'd borrow books from Timothy Whites Library or WH Smith's on Lord Street.

Occasionally you'd get a week out when you were not in a play so you just had daytime rehearsals and your nights free. I used to go to the cinema, there were seven in Southport then, and sometimes to the Garrick Theatre where they'd let you in at a discount if you had an Equity card.

Everything I ever learnt about acting came from Donald Bodley but he was very strict. We were not allowed to wear trousers or theatre make-up in the street. I was paid paid just £6 a week and were lucky to have a shilling left at the end of it.

We had to provide all our own costumes except for uniforms and period, which meant us rummaging for old skirts and jumpers in the market or at second hand shops like Percy Sutcliffe's in Market Street. Sometimes we'd buy new material from Ellwalds in Lord Street, near Rushtons Opticians, or Holmes in Tulketh Street, and make our own dresses. A lady called Joan got me cheap material in the sales at Broadbents. Bates in the Cambridge Arcade was an Aladdin's cave and sold dressmaking materials which we could sew up. We couldn't afford Marshall and Snelgrove's or Alexanders prices. Sometimes we swapped clothes because they looked different on other people. The audience would notice if you wore the same outfit twice within a few weeks.

We sat in Andy's coffee bar in Coronation Walk one morning and Eileen Derbyshire (Emily Nugent in 'Coronation Street') said to me, Oh Jean, do you think we'll be doing this for ever?' I said, "I hope not".

Along with other girls in the cast, Jean had to take her turn to be a judge at the popular English Rosebud competition.

The company stayed at the Scala until it was demolished in 1962. It is now part of Morrisons car park. They returned to the Casino for a few years until that in turn was demolished in 1970 having been deemed unsafe by the council.

However, Jean had already left the company in 1958, by which time audiences were dwindling, and she moved to York Repertory Company but by 1961, tired after ten years of the weekly grind of rep, she went to London and found an agent who could get her TV work. For the first year, parts were few and far between.

I got a couple of plays and a few Z-Cars episodes and I'd appeared in two episodes of Coronation Street in 1963, playing a landlady, Mrs Webb, when I was offered the part of Hilda Ogden in 1964. I was relieved to get out of London, which I hated.

Jean returned home to the family house in Sefton Street and, not being able to drive, commuted daily to Granada studios in Manchester by train. She left the house at 8am and didn't get back until 8.30pm at night.

Jean played Hilda for 23 years, becoming one of the best-known faces on television and, in 2006 at the age of 80, she is still enjoying a busy acting career, playing Auntie Wainwright in *Last of the Summer Wine*.

Off-screen, Jean is involved on the Macmillan Nurses committee and is a popular personality at local official functions.

PAT BALL

Pat Ball and her family have owned the Shelbourne Hotel on Lord Street for the past 25 years but the town's theatregoers probably know her best for her legendary performance as the Wicked Witch in the Southport Dramatic Club pantomimes. She is married to Norman and they have three children and four grandchildren.

In the early days of the Shelbourne, Sue & I were regular diners at the restaurant, where Pat made her celebrated recipe of Jambalaya especially for me, and for many years, I supplied the discos for functions at the hotel.

And, of course, I was a big fan of Pat's in the theatre although I preferred her costume in 'Lock Up Your Daughters' to the cloak of the Wicked Witch!

We sat in the hotel bar one afternoon in July 2006 and she told me her story.

I was born on January 23rd 1941 at Christiana Hartley Maternity Hospital. I went to St. Philip's School and then the Girls High School. We lived first in Meadow Avenue, Birkdale and then behind the Synagogue in Ball Street, which is now called Trinity Mews.

We had no bathroom but, once a week, my mother and I would go to the slipper bath in the Victoria Baths where they issued us with towels and, for a penny extra, a portion of bath oil. Our friends thought we were very posh as they made do with zinc baths in the kitchen.

As a child, I played on the islands in the Marine Lake and had great fun but now they're shut off because of the Health and Safety Act. We went on Gore's coach trips; to Pleasureland; Peter Pans Playground, where they had an Old English Sheepdog called Nana, and the Aquarium. I miss things like the Belle Vue Hotel, the Open Air Pool, the Land of the Little People and the Model Yacht Pond in Princes Park. All gone. When the Land of the Little People was demolished to make way for the ill-feted Sibec development, the council could have had the whole set-up for nothing but they didn't bother.

Every year there was a Pet Show at the Cambridge Hall for children to enter their hamsters, rabbits, budgies and other small creatures.

My mother, Marjorie Hall, kept a music library for Teddy Marks who ran orchestras in the area. He played at the old Casino on the Pier Head. They served tea on the terrace and Phil Java played the violin. He was the ladies' favourite. His brother, Harry's orchestra played on 'Those Were The Days'.

My first job was with the Ministry of Pensions and Insurance in Bootle when I was sixteen but I moved a year later to their office at 18 Waterloo Road by Grosvenor Road lights, a grand old house called Stoneycroft which has since been demolished whereupon we were moved to Duke's House in Hoghton Street. I married Norman in 1961.

In 1966, I got a night job as a croupier at the Kingsway Club working from 8pm to 3 or 4 a.m. and still had to be at Duke's House for nine. We wore full-length black skirts and white blouses which had to have high necks and buttoned sleeves to prevent us slipping money or chips down our cleavages or up our sleeves. I lasted nearly three years there. They called me 'the snooty blond' because I had my hair piled up in a beehive.

In 1971, Pat left the civil service and she and Norman bought Davies's toy and souvenir business in Neville Street, which they re-named The Friendly Dragon.

The cellars were part of the original underground Neville Street shops. Kids used to swarm up Neville Street and clear the shelves as they streamed through the shop. We made hardly any profit. We'd go for a meal at the Pony Express in Eastbank Street and spend the day's takings.

We used to sell these little coloured combs for 5d. each but 10d. if you wanted your name on them. I used to sit in the back with a tin of Airfix paint feverishly painting names. Airfix model kits were our best sellers, along with Sasha dolls.

In 1976, we sold the shop and bought a house in Winter Gardens Terrace for my mother, which she ran as holiday flats. In 1978, we bought the two next door and eventually we owned all six in the road, moving in and out of each one as we did them up. At one time, our two sons slept in tents in the garden in the summer to make room for the guests.

The Ball family's big move came in 1981 when they took over a Temperance guesthouse at the corner of Duke Street and Lord Street West called The Shelbourne.

There were ten bedrooms and only two bathrooms with coin slot meters on the showers. Breakfast was at 8.30 a.m. sharp and you had to choose your evening meal from the menu before you went out in the morning. There was just one sitting for dinner so, if you were late, you went without. Similarly, if you came in after ten at night, the doors were locked. How they ever got guests to return is a mystery.

Pat and Norman made immediate drastic changes to the hotel.

We converted all the bedrooms to en-suites, got a drinks licence and installed a bar, extended meal times and menus and gave guests their own front door key. Shortly afterwards, we bought the house next door, No.6 Duke Street, and linked it to the hotel, adding more bedrooms, enlarging the lounge and forming a small function suite.

When we bought No. 8 in 1989, we moved up to our current 23 bedrooms and built a new large function suite.

A couple of years ago, we bought Valentino's Italian restaurant across the road and that has proved to be very popular.

When we first bought the hotel, holidaymakers used to arrive at the Ribble Bus Station but, more recently, our guests have been businessmen and golfers. Many of the attractions, such as the Sea Bathing Lake, that brought families with children to a holiday resort have disappeared. We don't get many long stay holidaymakers but people do come in for special events like the Air Show, the Fireworks Display and the Flower Show. We also get a lot of people who are looking to buy property and move here.

Our son, Nigel, runs the bar and is famous for his guest beers while our other son, Philip, has the Berkley Hotel in Queens Road and two hotels in Hawkshead.

Pat's whole social life from being a little girl has centred round dance, song and drama.

As a little girl, my mother would take me to the theatre. I can remember bringing in the New Year at the Casino, on the Pier, in 1946. Later on, we went to shows there. There was a very steep rake on the stage. The artistes started the show at the back and ended up almost falling into the audience. Every time the Pier train went past, the building rattled and you couldn't hear what the actors were saying.

From the age of about nine, I used to go dancing with my mother in the Municipal Gardens in the afternoons to the music of bands like Jimmy Leech and his Organolians, Waldini, Edwin Harper plus various military bands playing in the old bandstand. It used to get packed.

I took dancing lessons with Betty Bersi who had a studio above the Cheshire Lines railway station on Lord Street.

The very day Pat told me this, plans were announced to turn that same building, which later had housed the Ribble Bus Station but had been empty for years, into a 96-room hotel. Let us hope it won't be another of Southport's grandiose schemes that comes to nothing like Sibec etc. Only time will tell.

But back to Pat.

I'd always loved the theatre. The first pantomime I saw was Norman Evans in Mother Goose at the Garrick Theatre.

I went to the North West School of Speech and Drama at 32 Roe Lane. It was started by Christabel Burniston and Jocelyn Bell and had over 100 students, many of them full-time. We put on many shows at the Little Theatre. I owe all my speech and drama training to them. They were brilliant. Christabel founded the English Speaking Board, which had its first headquarters at Roe Lane.

I joined the Southport Dramatic Club in 1958 and my first part was the daughter in Noel Coward's 'Nude with Violin'. When we did it recently, in 2003, I played the mother!. I have directed several plays for the S.D.C. over the years and guested with the Southport and Maghull operatic societies among others.

In 1984, I was involved in the British comedy film 'Mr. Love' that was shot in Hesketh Park and featured Maurice Denham.

And Pat's acting career has never been better.

I'm about to go on tour with a professional outfit called C'est Tous Theatre Company playing Madame Arcati in Noel Coward's 'Blithe Spirit', the part Margaret Rutherford played in the film. We're performing at open-air concerts at places like Sizergh Castle and Heskin Hall.

Meanwhile, Pat and Norman have had plans drawn up to convert the Shelbourne into luxury apartments although they are still continuing to run Valentinos.

We've had 25 years of very hard work, we thought it was time to relax. Norman likes playing golf and I can do more acting.

Sounds fair enough. And I look forward to seeing Pat return one Christmas as the Wicked Witch.

PHILIP BERRILL

Philip Berrill was born in Northampton in 1945. He moved to Southport in 1970 and has since made a name for himself in the town as a successful artist. His books and videos on painting sell all over the world. In the late 1990's, he was elected onto Sefton Council as a Conservative member. He is married to Sylvia. They have a daughter, Penny.

Philip Berrill is a genius for self-promotion. I can identify with that. People have said to me, 'You're in the paper more than bloody Philip Berrill,' but how else are self-employed entrepreneurs, for that is what Philip and I essentially are, to promote themselves?

Nonetheless, it is not always a popular characteristic as people confuse it with arrogance yet, more than ever nowadays, you have to go out there and sell yourself. There are many highly talented people who never make it because nobody hears about them.

People can't say they haven't heard about Philip but becoming an artist is not an easy road to success. It takes a lot of hard work as he assured me when I talked to him at his home near Hesketh Park.

I was eighteen when I held my first one-man art exhibition. It was in aid of Oxfam. When I first came to Southport, at the age of 25, I was in Retail Management. I took over as manager of Lonsdale International, which was a stationery store at the corner of Eastbank Street and Chapel Street where Blacks, the outdoor shop, is now.

I moved to McCabes, the electrical firm in Birkdale Village and, after that, I was manager at Cosmic Electrical Appliances in Marshside Road. Lancashire Co-op owned Cosmic and they had a branch in Chapel Street where Marks and Spencer is now. I stayed there until 19 when I left to set up as a professional artist.

All this time, Philip was spending all his spare time painting and making plans to launch himself as an artist. His first big step to this end was a one-man exhibition of his abstract paintings at Liverpool University in 1974 at the time of the famous John Moore's Biennale.

It was my version of the Edinburgh Fringe. Brian Redhead, the legendary broadcaster, opened it. He was editor of the Manchester Evening News at the time. The Southport Visiter put out a supplement cover featuring 'Philip – The Artist'. This started the ball rolling for me. I started running weekly classes at the YMCA in Hoghton Street.

Within two years, Philip was running national correspondence courses in painting and organising painting holidays.

In the mid-seventies, people began to have more money and more leisure time. My classes were increasing as more people enrolled. I was getting commissions, including a lot of murals which I enjoyed painting. In 1976, I had a long-playing record issued called 'Let's Learn to Paint'. It included watercolours and was sponsored by Winsor and Newton. It sold two and a half thousand copies

I took a lease on an old newsagents in Portland Street opposite the Prince of Wales Hotel and opened it up as an artist's' supplies shop and I also rented a former dance studio in Coronation Walk and turned it into a classroom at one side and an art gallery and studio in the other. The classes became incredibly popular.

These were the golden years. I had my own TV series, 'Paint with the Flying Artist'. I was organising painting holidays all over Europe and my books were published in numerous languages. The series was called 'Everyone's Guide to ….' and I called the company Philip Berrill International.

Always a good talker, Philip was able to turn his natural loquaciousness to his financial advantage.

I got into after dinner speaking when an agent called Bert Sharples, who operated from premises in Stanley Street, asked me to stand in one night when he'd been let down by a speaker at a venue in Blackburn. I wore a white suit with a red shirt and a red and blue spotted bow tie. I felt an entertainer should stand out. When I got there I found out I was there in place of Sir Anthony Hopkins. Most times, I painted as I talked and, at the end, I'd hand out free raffle tickets and the winner could keep the painting.

The recession at the end of the 1980's saw many small local shops facing closure and Philip realised his business was at a crossroads.

I knew I would have to expand or give up the shop. What really killed it was when Sefton Council brought in Pay and Display. It was a crazy idea, especially for a resort like Southport. Trade dipped everywhere. People were not prepared to pay for a five-minute stop-off for a quick purchase. I was lucky enough to sell the lease. The people who bought it opened as a designer dress shop but they didn't last long and eventually closed due to the economic circumstances of the time.

I concentrated on the teaching, my own paintings and the talks.

An inveterate letter writer to both the Visiter and the Champion on local affairs, it was no surprise that Philip became involved in local politics. He was invited to stand for the Conservatives on Sefton Council. He regarded himself as 'an independent right of centre'.

Councillor Jim Hayes, who was Mayor of Sefton, asked me if I'd be interested in standing in Ainsdale Ward. It was after the Conservatives had lost the general election by the biggest margin of seats ever. They were desperate for candidates. I told them that if I accepted, I intended to win. They were surprised at my confidence. They didn't expect a victory but I'd no intention of taking the job on to lose, and I didn't lose.

Philip won the seat in the May by 68 votes, the only seat in Sefton to change hands at that election. He began writing a column in the *Southport Champion* called 'New Kid On The Block'. This described his work on the council plus his comments about events in the town..

I rate keeping Ainsdale Police Station open as my greatest achievement in politics whilst my biggest disappointment was the demolition of the old Odeon Cinema on Lord Street, where Sainsbury's now stands.

I resigned in 2001. I wasn't happy with the way Sefton were doing things. There was a £5 million overspend on projects like Bootle New Baths and Ocean Plaza. Under the new cabinet government, 66 local councillors were to be paid an average of £6,000 per person and the full cost of council members rose from £330,000 to around £800,000. Many people struggle to pay their council tax yet some council cabinet member were being paid £15,000-£24,000a year. I was not happy with that situation.

Philip is known as 'The Flying Artist' due to his worldwide sketching and painting expeditions, especially for corporate clients. He still runs his popular Art Classes. Indeed, my wife and I have been to them but, after several months attendance, I don't think Jack Vettriano or Beryl Cook have anything to fear from either of us.

However, Philip has recently pulled off a big deal for his books in China so maybe I should quickly start buying a few of his original paintings before the rest of the world catches on.

WALLY BIRCH

Wally Birch was born in Waterloo on June 7th 1936. He is a founder member of Southport Squash club and now owns the Victoria Sports and Leisure Club. He lives in Freshfield with his wife Jess.

When we are out walking our dogs on Formby beach early in the morning, we occasionally see Wally out with his dog. He lives on the edge of the pinewoods and red squirrels were playing in his front garden when I called to see him in February 2006.

I attended Christ Church Boys School at Waterloo but left at fourteen and a half to be a shipping clerk in Liverpool until 1954 when I was called up and joined the R.E.M.E. I had various sales jobs from 1957 to 1990 by which time I was Field Sales Manager for The Toiletry Company (Part of B.A.T.).

In 1976, the Victorian swimming baths on the Promenade, built in 1839, were closed down and new baths were built on Dukes Way. At the time, I was a member of the Crosby Northern Club.

Myself and a number of fellow members could see potential in the old baths which were owned by the council and had been designated a Grade II Listed Building. At one time there had been an underground entry from the Baths to the old Promenade underpass but it had been bricked up due to falling debris.

We thought we could create a club of our own there and so we made an offer to lease the premises. No less than 400 of us formed a breakaway group and we went ahead with the lease, financed by a lifelong membership scheme with the aid of a grant from the Council. We called it Southport Squash Club and opened in 1978. The idea was that the new club would be self-financing with the bar takings and court fees.

The building included a section of the old baths, which we converted to squash courts, but we also opened the old birdie bath, financed by extra contributions. This proved to be our downfall as the maintenance costs of the pool exceeded all expectations. We managed to survive for ten years but, as squash declined in popularity, we found ourselves in debt.

To raise the cash, thirty-six people put in the extra money for which they received shares and a new club, The Victoria Sports Club, was formed. A committee of three was set up to run the operation, myself, John Turner and Rob Frobisher. For the first time, we introduced annual membership fees.

After two years, we decided the only way forward was to run the club as a purely commercial organisation and, on a vote, I became the sole owner in 1991.

I opened a gym, which we called The Tone Zone, which was run by my daughter, Sonia. We were one of the first, if not the first, in the area to introduce monitored induction whereby members were tested for their capability to use the different equipment.

We created an aerobics room for pilates and yoga and installed a sports bar. We had the birdie bath and four squash courts with four teams in the area squash leagues.

Wally also introduced a social side to the club with a Golf Society, Rambling Club, visits to the Theatre and quiz nights. Thirteen years after Southport Squash Club was formed, 118 out of the original 400 were still members.

Our only competition in the leisure club business at the time was from the Royal Clifton and the Stutelea Hotels. Later, Brent Sherman opened The Train Station in the old West Lancs Squash Club premises.

Ours was a family business. As well as Sonia running the gym, our son, Peter was the club secretary and accountant and, when we opened up at Formby, our other daughter Sue, became the receptionist.

The Formby branch, in The Cloisters above Somerfields in Formby Village, opened in 1990 in what used to be 6,000 square feet of offices. It has full gym facilities including a ladies gym, with steam, sauna and therapy rooms but no swimming pool.

As time went on, we expanded in Southport. The old Ladies First Class Plunge pool was buried underneath the four squash courts. The demand for squash had dropped off so we scrapped the courts and resurrected the old pool, turning it into an 18-metre pool and a hydro learner pool with two steam rooms. We then built an extension at the back to accommodate two squash courts and two saunas and two steam baths.

By now, the club covered an area of 30,000 square feet and had 2700 members with another 800 in Formby. In 2001, Wally leased the building at the corner of Neville Street and the Promenade.

Previously the Garcia family had run it as the Casa Garcia Restaurant and function room. When they left, it became an Irish pub called O'Tooles but, by the time I bought it, the place had been derelict for five years. We completely renovated it and opened as QV's, a wine/café bar serving meals downstairs and a function room upstairs. The bar alone cost £3,000.

Unfortunately, it wasn't the success I'd hoped and after twelve months, I let it out on a franchise.

QV's, under new stewardship, became The Fuzzy Peach nightclub for a short time but there was competition on the doorstep because, situated in the building between Wally's leisure club and QV's, there was another nightclub, one that changed hands periodically. I remember D.J.-ing there in the 70's when Clive Slater, who owned a thriving Portakabin business, ran it as Royales with topless barmaids. During Wally's time alone it had been called Palm Court, Manhattans, Infinity and Havana.

The franchise didn't really work out and I ended up selling the business to Stephen Kelly who has turned it into a sports bar with 14 TV screens. They call it the CU Bar and show live Premiership football on a Saturday afternoon.

Despite a quadruple by-pass operation a year ago, Wally has made a full recovery and is still in charge of the Victoria Sports Club.

During the last fourteen years, we have spent over one and a half million pounds in added facilities and refurbishment including a new fitness studio, new ladies and gents gymnasiums, children's' drop-in centre and a sports bar.

A keen sportsman, Wally also does a great deal to help Southport FC by offering the players the full facilities of his gym for training.

MICHAEL BRAHAM

A man involved in many aspects of public life in Southport, Michael Braham was actually born on April 30th 1949 in Bolton but his family moved to Southport when he was 18 months old. He is a partner at Brighouses solicitors, a leading member of the Jewish community and a Deputy Lieutenant of Merseyside. He lives in Birkdale with his wife, Sue, and children Alexander and Victoria.

I have known Michael for many years through my connections with Southport Football Club as he is the club's historian.

He also a partner at Brighouses, who are my own solicitors, although I have had no dealings with him in that role which is just as well as he specialises in crime and divorce and, happily, I have been not yet been involved in either.

My Dad, Danny, opened a ladies fashion shop in Bolton in 1938 and expanded until he owned a chain over thirty shops all over the North of England but in 1950, he moved to Southport as he thought it a more salubrious place to live and bring up a family..

We lived for a while at the old Belle Vue Hotel until we found a house to buy, at 2 Selworthy Road. I went to Sunnymede School, which in 1954 was at 40 Grosvenor Road but is now situated at 2 Westcliffe Road, at what was once Wybourne Gate, a home for disabled ex-servicemen. The headmaster, Mr. O.P. Beachey, was a disciplinarian. Even the youngest boys were caned if they misbehaved and from the age of six we had drill on the lawn, marching like miniature soldiers.

From thirteen to eighteen, I went to Clifton College in Bristol. I used to get Wednesday's Southport Journal and the Lancashire Evening Football Post sent down to me every week. The 'It is Whispered That...' gossip column, aimed at teenagers, had transferred from the defunct Guardian to the Journal so I was able to keep up with events in the town amongst my peers, as well as following the local sport.

I did my law training at College of Law in Chester. My first job was as an articled clerk in Manchester for £4 a week. I used to catch the 7.55am train (The 9am service was known as 'The Gentleman's Train'), which cost £2.14.0d. (£2.70p.) for a weekly ticket, an appreciable part of my salary. To supplement my income, I served writs for ten and sixpence a time. Once I served one on a butcher who had a stall on Wigan Market but, when I handed him the writ, he took it from me and calmly wrapped it up with some sausages that he sold to the lady behind me in the queue.

My first job on qualifying was in Blackburn but Milton Mannheim, a larger than life character known as 'Southport's Rumpole', headhunted me in January 1982 and I became a partner in Mannheim, Otto and Braham.

After five happy years there, I became a partner at Brighouses, when Stuart Fish left to become a District Judge. I became Head of the Criminal Department, specialising in Matrimonial Law.

Brighouses was started in 1882 by Samuel (later Sir Samuel) Brighouse who was the coroner for West Lancashire for 56 years. I believe he was the last elected coroner in the country. One could only vote in Ormskirk so he used to pay half a crown to anyone who wanted to vote for him, which also covered the cost of a meal. He died in 1940 at the age of ninety having conducted a staggering 20,000 inquests.

Another of Southport's great legal characters was Benny Hartwell who was Clerk of the Magistrates Court. He once asked a defendant, whom he had found guilty, what was in the brown paper bag he was carrying. 'A pair of shoes I've just bought from Timpsons,' the man replied. 'Well take them back and get them to refund your money,' ordered Benny. 'Knock off sixpence for your bus fare and bring the rest of it here to pay your fine.'

My main concern at the moment is that the North Sefton Magistrates Court, which was the Southport Magistrates Court until 1974, will be moved to Bootle. It was tried once before but we successfully fought against it. I feel very strongly that people who have committed crimes locally should be tried locally. The Court was built in 1940 on the site of the old KGV School at Woodlands, before it moved to Scarisbrick New Road.

I asked Michael if he had any interesting stories about any of his cases and he promptly brought out twelve bulging scrapbooks filled with cuttings not only from his court appearances but treasured souvenirs of the minutia of his life. I realised I needed a month to absorb them all.

I defended the burglar who was badly beaten up by Everton footballer, Duncan Ferguson, when he caught him breaking into his Freshfield home. I advised him he could ask the police to charge Ferguson for assault as it appeared he had used unnecessary violence (the law says you are allowed to use reasonable force to DEFEND yourself) but it turned out he was an Everton fan with the footballer's name tattooed on his arm. Had he known it was Ferguson's house, he wouldn't have dreamt of stealing from his hero.

I was on Ferguson's side on this one. No wonder crime is so rife in this country today. Who is the victim here? But I digress.

Michael is known for his wit in court as in the case of the man recently prosecuted for trying to sell a stuffed owl on e-bay.

I told the court that the defendant took the matter very seriously. It wasn't that he didn't give a hoot.

Or the man who attacked his neighbour in a Southport flat.

I pointed out my client was a normally a gentle man although I admit his use of the words "I'll cut your jugular from ear to ear" might have been considered threatening.

Now I know why Michael is such a popular and successful after dinner speaker. His political career, however, has been less successful.

Seven times I've put up for the council as a Liberal in Dukes Ward where I live, from the days when it was Birkdale West, but I've never been elected. That ward had once been considered a 'rotten borough' having returned an unopposed Tory for 34 years between 1912 and 1946. I first stood in 1971. Both myself and my opponent, Lawrence Vaughan-Williams, were only 21. The previous time the ward had been contested, in 1967, the Tories had commandeered 92.7% of the vote. I managed to achieve 30%. Joyce Charlton, the matriarch of the local Conservative Association, told me I had fought a dirty campaign for 'having the cheek to stand'!

I put up for Parliament twice as well, but they were both hopeless causes. I am very fond of supporting hopeless causes. I stood against Harold Wilson at Huyton in 1974, when Wilson was at his zenith as Prime Minister, and I lost my deposit, as did another of his opponents at a previous election, one Screaming Lord Sutch, so I was in good company.

I lost it again in 1979 standing for Preston North, which was another safe Labour seat. The local Liberal Association decided not to contest the seat and I was unable to get time off work so I canvassed on my own on my free evenings, with little help from the local party. I was amazed that 2715 people voted for me.

After I lost at Huyton, Harold Wilson invited me to join the Labour party, confessing that he himself had once been a member of the Oxford University Liberal Club until he 'saw the light'.

However, I did become Chairman of the Southport Liberal party from 1980-82 and President of the Southport Liberal Democrats 1998-2000 and was proud of the part I played in helping Ronnie Fearn win back the seat for the Liberals after 63 years of Tory domination from 1924-1987.

In 1985, Michael wrote a booklet on the history of the local party entitled 'The Southport Liberal Association – The First 100 Years' but it is for his other learned tome that he is best known.

'The Sandgrounder – The Complete History of Southport Football Club in the Football League' was written in collaboration with the club's statistician, Geoff Wilde.

I had the idea of writing a series of articles on old players for the Southport Visiter, Geoff had a similar interest and it mushroomed into this giant project whereby we interviewed over 650 ex-players, or the families of those who had died. It took 20 years of research travelling all over the country. Geoff retired in 1991 so had the time to travel abroad to see all those players who had emigrated. It then took us another three years to write the book, which was eventually published in 1995. It is now long out of print but the odd copy pops up from time to time on e-bay and fetches in the region of £120.

For me, writing the book was a pure labour of love. I'd supported the club since I was eight years old when I saw them lose to Wigan Athletic 2-1 in the F.A. Cup in 1957. I've been a shareholder and Vice President of the club for many years.

I'm also a big cricket fan and a member of Southport & Birkdale Cricket Club and the M.C.C.

A prominent member of the Jewish community in Southport, Michael is a trustee and the archivist and historian of the Southport Hebrew Congregation. He is also an executive member of Southport's Association of Jewish Ex-Servicemen and the Honorary Secretary of the Southport Hebrew Philanthropic Society.

Southport's first synagogue was opened in 1893 and was housed in what is now the Talbot Hall in Sussex Road and the current home of the Wings Club. The Arnside Road building was consecrated in 1926 and the Amelan Hall behind it was built in 1955. There is also have a Reform Synagogue in Portland Street as well one at the Jewish Old Age Home in Albert Road.

During the War, due to evacuation, there was a large influx of Jewish people into the town, the number rising from about 500 to over 3000. Over the passage of time, this number has declined considerably. Over the years, a lot of Jewish people have drifted back to Manchester, Liverpool and London, possibly because there are no Jewish schools in the town.

Many of the original family-run shops on Lord Street, which gave the street its unique exclusivity, were owned by Jewish families. At one time, there must have been 20-30 ladies fashion shops along the street but high rents and competition from the multiples has driven nearly all of them away.

The furriers, in which shops like Fletchers, Lawrences and Koe-Bels were leading lights in the town, have all but disappeared, doubtless affected by the animal rights movements.

Michael has been involved in the Birkdale Civic Society, Queenscourt Hospice and the Southport Pier Trust but his proudest achievement is to be appointed a Deputy Lieutenant of Merseyside.

There are 30 of us in Lancashire, two in Southport, myself and Air Commodore Jack Broughton. The original purpose of the deputies was to press gang men into the Forces in time of war but now the role is purely ceremonial.

Michael is a very well-known figure in the town, not least for his eccentric dress sense. I have seen him at football matches sporting a T-shirt and South African bush hat one week and a bow tie and straw hat the next.

He is involved in so many things in a town in which, he says, he is so proud to live and work, that there is no event I might attend where I would be surprised to see him.

TONY BROTHWELL

Tony Brothwell has tuned pianos in Southport for the past fifty years. He was born in Sidcup, Kent on Sept 29th 1939.

Tony has been a regular visitor to my house, tuning my various pianos, since the sixties. As piano tuning has never been an overcrowded profession, I knew he would have a unique slant on events in the town.

My family moved to Southport when I was eight months old because my father was with the Land Registry and he was transferred from London to Smedley Hydro. We lived in Dinorwic Road and I went to school at Bury Road, Farnborough Road and, finally, Birkdale Secondary Modern.

As a teenager, I went to St.John's Youth Club in Birkdale where we had ballroom dancing lessons with Mrs. Wheeler and a drama group. I was a chorister at the church.

In 1955, Frank Marshall, vicar of St. John's, wanted to build a daughter church in Carr Lane, to be called St.Mary's, but subscriptions didn't run to it and they had to settle for a hall which was used as a worship centre for about twenty years before it was finally demolished. A later vicar called it 'Marshall's Folly'.

I left school at fifteen and joined a firm called Henry Wills in Liverpool as an apprentice organ builder. Every Friday, we went along to Liverpool Cathedral to tune the organ there.

After just a year, I moved to Aldridges music shop in Hoghton Street. Most of their work was in selling, repairing and renovating pianos although they also sold televisions, radios, radiograms, sheet music and records.

In the 1950's, I started tuning pianos, learning the trade from the senior tuners. At that time, Aldridges employed four full-time tuners who each carried out an average of 27 jobs every week. They had contracts to tune pianos in school and hospitals.

Every Monday afternoon, I used to go to the Palace Hotel to tune their pianos, one in the ballroom and one in the restaurant where Al Chinnery played to the diners.

Once they found a piano locked in a storeroom at the end of the Pier, well after the Pier Bar closed down. I went along in a Force Nine gale but when I opened the lid, the strings shot out like they'd been catapulted. The sea air had corroded everything.

Once at the Garrick Theatre, the tabs split and lead shot that had been holding down the curtains flew out and peppered the piano. And when they showed films there midweek, some of the boisterous patrons would throw peanuts at the screen which fell into the piano if the lid was left open and it was a nightmare getting them all out.

The Arts Centre held a lot of excellent recitals in the seventies and I was often called out to tune their piano for virtuosos like John Lill and Peter Katin to play.

The finest pianos were Steinways and Bechsteins and many of Southport's largest houses boasted grand pianos. I called them my gracious ladies in elegant houses. However, by the 1930's, baby grands were becoming more popular as the houses that were being built then were not large enough to accommodate the grands. And, of course, as pianos are a good guide too social class, the poorer people bought uprights, as much as a furniture item as a musical one.

There used to be a thriving British piano building industry in the twenties and thirties, with names like Chappell, Hopkinson, Rogers and Broadwood, but that's all gone now. Instead we have the cheaper foreign imports from the Far East with names like, Kawai, and Samick. Yet their quality is good and Yamaha manufacture some of the finest instruments made today. The tuning pins on many modern pianos are difficult to turn as they are inserted by compressed air guns.

Aldridges closed in 1970 and Rumbelows took over the premises. Tony went freelance, continuing to service the instruments of many of Aldridges old customers.

Now, as far as I know, there is only myself and another piano tuner in Ainsdale left in the town. I tune about thirty pianos a week.

As well as private houses, I tune pianos in theatres, church halls, hotels, nursing homes and, of course, organs in churches. Wymott Prison is on my list and I managed to get 800 copies of the Gideon Bible in there. When Barbara Dix had her Academy of Music in Talbot Street, she had four pianos, two uprights and two grands of which one was a superb Steinway Model B.

Business has decreased over the years for various reasons but the main one is technology. People buy electric pianos and keyboards in preference to pianos as they do many more things and you can play them in privacy with headphones. Yet you can't beat a real piano though for sound quality. The piano has soul. The best piano in Southport today is a Steinway Model D concert grand which is at the Arts Centre.

I asked Tony the obvious question, what famous people have you tuned pianos for?

Hundreds. Whenever an important artist comes to town, they stipulate the provision of a perfectly tuned piano. Quite often they will insist a particular instrument is brought in.

Next week, Michael Ball is coming to Victoria Park to appear in the Summer Classics and a piano will have to be taken there. I will have to be present to make sure it is set up and tuned properly.

I was always disappointed that I was too young to tune Paul Robeson's piano but I tuned one for Tommy Steele when he came to the Garrick in pantomime in 1958.

When Pat Boone was on the Southport Theatre, the rear leg of the piano collapsed and we had to prop it up on a chair and drape a cloth over it so the audience wouldn't notice.

But Tony doesn't just tune the instruments, he plays them as well.

I had piano lessons from Brian Trueman and Wilfred Clayton. who was the organist at St. James's Church, between 1968 and 1973 and passed my music diploma. In 1965, I became the organist at St. Andrew Church in Eastbank Street, now replaced by the Job Centre.

When St. Andrews combined with Christ Church in 1970, I moved to St. Cuthbert's for ten years after which I lessened my load by stepping down to become assistant organist. And in 1985 I retired, but I still take the occasional booking although the decline of church weddings has meant much less work for the itinerant organist.

Before leaving, Tony was able to inform me that my own upright piano, which I fondly believed was a distinguished German make, was in fact Chinese or Korean but had been called Otto Bruening to give the illusion of European craftsmanship.

TONY CAFFERKEY

Tony Cafferkey was born in County Mayo on January 10th 1949. After graduating from Hoteliers Catering College in Ireland, he came over to England and worked in hotels in Scotland, the Midlands and the North before joining the Scarisbrick Hotel in 1972.

As a DJ in the 70's, I performed regularly at numerous functions in the Scarisbrick Hotel and that is when I first met Tony Cafferkey. Unlike most managers who told me to turn the sound down, Tony always wanted it turned up. He liked a lively hotel.

Now, three decades later, I was interviewing him in the hotel boardroom. A waiter brought tea and biscuits on a silver tray as we talked about his life in Southport.

I was working for Berni Inns in Manchester when I applied for the post of manager at the Scarisbrick Hotel and was offered the job. It was 1972 but I was only here a year because in 1973 I got married to Sylvia and we moved up to Scotland where I spent five years in Glasgow managing five hotels for the EMI Group. In 1978, EMI sold out to Thistle and I came back to the Scarisbrick in the October of that year as Chief Executive of the hotel.

The hotel had become run down and was in dire need of a cash injection to bring it back to its former glory. The owners, the Careys, found financial backers who would buy the freehold, which would then enable them to borrow money to renovate the building. But Frank Carey was not an hotelier and the lenders made a proviso that a professional manager had to be in charge of the operation if the deal was to go ahead. That was me. We were the first hotel to fast forward float on the Ofex trading market and raised £1 million to fund the building work. Shares were bought by individuals as well as venture capitalists.

The hotel had declined into a struggling 2-star establishment but we set the renovation in motion. Instead of aiming at the tourist market. couples from Canada spending a week in the town never to return, I set out to cater for local people and businesses who lived and worked here the whole year round.

People were sceptical. Michael Montrone, who was managing director of the Bold Hotel at the time, told me, 'You'll never make a success of that place, it's the pits'. I proved him wrong. Within two years, our ground floor bars, the Vic, the Avenue, the Barons and the Foghorn, were the busiest in Southport.

The money we made from the bars enabled us to refurbish the bedrooms. We went on to acquire pubs in Burscough, Euxton and Preston but these were sold off in the 1980's.

We had Lawrence Isherwood, the artist, living at the hotel in the early seventies. He paid his bill for bed and breakfast with paintings. We had so many, we renamed the main function room The Isherwood Suite and hung some of them in there hoping he'd become a sought after name and we'd cash in but it hasn't happened yet.

In 1989, the Scarisbrick celebrated its centenary with a civic dinner at the hotel but it was also the year that Frank Carey severed connections with the hotel. Tony, together with Mrs Carey, headed a management buy out of the hotel. This eventually led to exciting expansion plans.

There were garages at the back of the hotel that had been the original stables in the olden days when the hotel was a coaching inn. They became twelve new bedrooms. In the early nineties, we added another ten bedrooms in what had previously been staff accommodation.

In 1992, we created Maloney's Bar out of the old pool room and the Avenue bar. It was an instant success. There had been nothing like it in the town before. It was very upmarket. We served over 250 varieties of cocktails and the bartenders were performers, imitating Tom Cruise in the film 'Cocktail'.

The concept was so successful that between 1999 and 2004 we opened up Maloney's in Wigan, Bolton, St. Helens and Oldham at a cost of up to half a million each.

In the late-90's, we knocked down some old shops and a cottage in Scarisbrick Avenue and West Street to build an extension that housed fifteen more bedrooms; a new function room, which we called the Barker Suite, and a leisure centre with a 15 meter swimming pool, gym, steam rooms and sauna. We turned the old paint shop and wine cellars into a restaurant we called Cloisters. All these we opened in time for the Millennium.

When new licensing laws were planned for 2005, opening the door to 24 hour drinking, Tony had to make certain decisions regarding the running of the businesses in the light of the changes. One of those decisions was to dispose of the out of town Maloney's bars.

Opening longer hours greatly increased running costs as the bars had to be manned as long as we were open. The problems were elongated. At the Scarisbrick, we decided to close at one a.m. as there were numerous nightclubs and discos all around us in West Street and Waverley Street to cater for the all-night trade.

Alongside running the hotel, Tony has always been involved in community work linked to the tourist industry.

In the early eighties, I was a founder director and member of the Sefton Marketing Bureau set up to encourage the local authority to improve marketing of the area. It worked, too, as the council found the money to employ two marketing gurus to promote day visitors and conferences. I was vice-chairman of the North West Tourist Board for 15 years, until the government abolished it, and I became a director of its successor, the Merseyside Tourist Board.

Tony was also a member, and is a life vice-president, of the Southport Flower Show board.

In 1987, the show was almost defunct. The council washed its hands off it. We got rid of all the ancillary stuff and went back to basis with horticulture as the dominant theme. We are now a registered company with charitable status and Victoria Park has been upgraded. The show is now healthier and better attended than it ever was, and without the show jumping and the dog shows. Now it's second only to Chelsea Flower Show and I'm proud to be part of it.

After decades of boarding house closures and private hotels being converted to flats and rest homes, plans for two new hotels have been put forward for the Town Centre, one on the site of the old Palace Cinema and one in the Floral Hall Gardens. I asked Tony how he viewed the new competition.

There have been lots of proposals over the years but none have been built so far. The Floral Hall one will be an adjunct to their Conference trade whilst Vincents is aimed at a niche market.

Tony told me his main hobby was golf.

I came late to the sport and consider myself fortunate to be accepted as a member of Hillside Golf Club but I also go back to Ireland to play at my hometown club at Belmullet where I am still a member.

I'm also a big football fan and in 2005 the hotel hosted the civic ceremony to commemorate Southport's promotion from the Conference North to the Nationwide Conference.

Tony did admit to me that he was also a Liverpool supporter but I gently suggested to him that, knowing how keen he is to support local events, he might transfer his allegiance to Southport.

I look forward to his appearance at Haig Avenue next season with bated breath.

MARTIN CONNARD

Born in Southport on May 19th 1948, Martin Connard runs the oldest family business still operating in Lord Street, the famous jewellers shop founded by his grandfather, Walter Connard, in 1883.

I interviewed Martin one Tuesday morning in May 2006 and entering his shop was an incredible experience, like stepping back in time. Everything was the same as it had been in Victorian days. His wife, Janet, brought out tea and custard crèmes as Martin told me the remarkable story of his ancestors and about his own life in Southport.

My grandfather, Walter, was born in 1859 but his grandmother was born in a cottage on Lord Street where the Atkinson Art Gallery stands today so our Southport roots go back a long way.

The family at that time were builders and in the 1881 census, grandfather was listed as a master builder employing 48 men and 6 boys.

He opened the jewellers shop with his brother, Arthur. It was a single storey building with a garden alongside but he had the foresight to buy up the land from here to the corner and back to Stanley Street and he built The Masonic Building which was the first three-storey building north of Neville Street. The freemasons occupied the top floors for their meetings before they moved to Duke Street.

Originally there was an arcade alongside our shop. Grandfather wanted to open a cinema here and plans were passed but he eventually built the Palladium across the road instead, on the site of Haughton House. He also commissioned The Mermaid Fountain, which is still there today, although the wonderful cinema has been replaced by Sainsbury's.

So Martin followed his father, Charles, into the business.

I was educated first at Churchtown primary school until I was 11 when I went to Croxton in Park Crescent, one of the many private schools in Southport. It's now a block of flats called Croxton Court.

We called it the 'tiddlywink school because of the red tiddlywinks on the blue caps. There were about 70 boys there in my time, some of them boarders. Mr. Howell was the headmaster; a disciplinarian. We had sports every afternoon; football, cricket, hockey and swimming. Those boys who didn't have push bikes and didn't want to walk to the baths, he would drive down and charge them a penny each. He'd been known to get as many as twenty boys crammed in his car. We had to do our homework at school between 6 and 7.30pm before we went home which I liked as, once you were home your time was your own.

I was only there for two years whereupon I passed for Merchant Taylor's in Crosby where I got my 'A' levels in maths, physics and chemistry then came straight into the family business in 1966.

Martin embarked on a two-year evening course at Liverpool and became a Fellow of the Gemmological Association of Great Britain. I was very impressed with his vast knowledge of gems and soon realised that I would never make a jeweller as, not only am I colour blind but I was unable to distinguish between a £50 diamond and a £5,000 one. He went on to tell me about the course.

There were sixty people on the first night but it dwindled to about forty as many did not realise how much work was involved. Yet it was a most enjoyable course and not only for jewellers. There were people who just wanted to learn about crystallography and gems.

In those days, there were only six or seven jewellers in Southport whereas now there are over thirty yet, alas, fewer craftsmen with specialist skills. For example, most of the engravers still around are in their 50's and 60's. In the Birmingham jewellery quarter you would have had several tradesmen in one building, each pursuing a different craft, but now a lot of skills have been lost and whilst we sell mostly fine quality English-made jewellery from small family firms, there is a big importation of jewellery from overseas, particularly the Far East.

Most shops today have all their stock records on their computers with few of them keeping records of past sales. We have a record of most pieces of jewellery that passes over our counter, going back to Victorian times. We know who bought it, when sold and sometimes even a diagram of the design.

Aside from his jewellery business, Martin is also President of the Southport and District Temperance Society.

I was invited to be President in 1993. I turned it down at first but the Chairman, Albert Hopkins, persuaded me to take it on. I try to be a very active President, not just a figurehead. I've hardly missed a meeting. We have 30-40 members keeping the flag flying but the recent change in the licensing laws, permitting 24-hour opening, means the drinking culture in England is increasing. Everyone accepts the problems alcohol causes but, so far, few people want to promote temperance. The society started in 1836 and at one time owned The Albert in London Street as a Temperance Hotel.

Our London Street building is a fine one and during the last twelve years has had extensive restoration work carried out which, due to its size, is always on-going.

The Hindley Family in particular are stalwarts of the Society and do a lot of good work. rented out to various organisations such as. The dance floor is a sprung one, taken up from the old Palais de Danse on Lord Street, and is used regularly by many organisations, groups and musical societies like the Maureen Jeffrey School of Dance and the Southport Amateur Operatic Society and the Birkdale Orpheus.

We have a stand every year at the Southport Carnival.

One of Martin's other hobbies was racing pigeons.

I had always liked birds and used to help Albert Cadwell at the Botanic Gardens aviaries. He and his father, Jimmy, were very keen pigeon fanciers and I started going round to their lofts, watching the excitement of birds coming home on race days. I soon started with my own birds, joining the High Park Homing Society.

We used to mark (ie release the pigeons) from the old Hesketh Park Station. There were about 15 members but the club closed in 1965 and I moved to the Marshside Flying Club, which marked from the Bold Arms in Churchtown. It's still going today.

The boundaries of the different clubs are dictated by the prevailing wind and the birds fly at speeds of up to 80-90 mph.

The area bounded by Moss Lane, Warren Road, Devonshire Road and Old Park lane was known as Little Belgium and at one time there were over fifty lofts there. My first big win was the 1966 Southport and Birkdale Open Young bird race from Newhaven when 128 fanciers sent 466 birds and my nominated red chequer hen, 'Newhaven Queen', won by ten minutes which was well in front because so many races are won at the home end with say a group of three or four flying together and then it is who can trap their pigeon first to remove the rubber race ring and record it in the pigeon clock who wins.

I became fascinated by the long distance racing and joined the British Barcelona Club (864 miles) being delighted to have one of my birds return home. Likewise in my last race I topped Marshside with my nominated bird and thought it was a nice way to finish. I don't know how I ever found the time for all the training and hours spent but it was all thoroughly enjoyable and with so many delightful characters.

My other interests include fishing, course and fly-fishing for trout along with setting lines on the shore with Mick Johnson and Ian Beecham. We would make up two lines, each with a hundred hooks on and stake them out at low tide, then follow the tide out and it was exciting to seen what you had caught. One time when nearer to Lytham pier than Southport, we had eight Bass, which was a special treat.

I have always supported Southport F. C. and in the 1970's I was on the Special Events Committee. We had all the big names in football like Bill Shankly, Alan Ball Snr, Joe Mercer and Tommy Docherty for the Sportsman's Dinners, and had some success in raising money for the Club. It would be nice to think more people from Southport supported them because there are some excellent games to be seen there.

As a family we have all loved the shop which is why my grandfather was still coming down working at 86, my Aunt Georgiana at 91 and both my parents, Charles and Helen, in their late 80's and with our son Andrew continuing and if the good Lord is kind I hope to also be coming down at a similar age – only time will tell.

I asked Martin what gave him the most satisfaction and enjoyment from his business and he said it was working with his wife, family and pleasant staff; seeing and handling all the beautiful pieces and having so many delightful customers of all ages who love coming to us and pay us such nice compliments.

'A fine sentiment,' I replied to the President of the Temperance Society. 'I'll drink to that'.

EDWARD CROWHURST

Edward Crowhurst is a wheelwright and bodger and is one of the few surviving links with Southport's agricultural and rural beginnings. He was born at Moss Cottage on Martin Mere on June 6th 1927 and has lived in the Crossens and Churchtown area all his life.

I didn't know what a bodger was until I met Edward at his workshop in four acres of land out in Banks. It was July 2006 but, out there on the moss, it could just as easily have been 1930.

Moss Cottage was at the end of New Lane in Crossens, towards Three Pools, so I went to St. John's in Crossens, which was the nearest school. It was about a mile and a half walk and I went there until I was fourteen. When the War started, a lot of evacuees arrived in Crossens and extra classes were held in the Methodist hall and in a room above the Co-op.

My father was foreman for Scarisbrick Estates and my mother was a tailor at Bobbie's in Lord Street making Masonic robes and made-to-measure suits. Bobbie's was a very high-class shop and later became Marshall & Snelgroves and now Debenhams.

As a lad, all my social life was spent round the farms, cycling, taking horses out and meeting in the pubs although I did join the scouts at St. John's when I was ten and a couple of times I went to the youth club at the Methodist Church. In the holidays, we went Youth Hostelling.

I played the trombone in the Banks Brass Band from when I was fifteen. We performed at church fetes, Meols Hall, schools and at the Crossens Festival. In 1945, we played at the Welcome Home party in Banks for our servicemen returning from the War.

I played the trombone in the Southport Youth Orchestra at the Cambridge Hall and six of us formed a little ensemble. We used to practice in the Volunteer pub in Eastbank Street.

I got married at Churchtown Congregational Church in 1951. My parents had once been caretakers there, stoking up the Robin Hood boilers.

So how did Edward become a wheelwright instead, perhaps, of playing in a jazz orchestra?

I've always worked with wood. I started as a joiner's apprentice in 1941 at J.D. Wilkinson's in Forest Road, the firm that built Crossens Library. Mr. Wilkinson was an alderman and ex-Mayor of Southport. There was another firm, in Crossens, called the Tomlinson's, that built the school and church there.

Wilkinson closed the business down during the War and, in 1944, I went to work for his ex-foreman, John Rimmer, who bought a yard in Sussex Road and started a joinery and undertaking business. Many joiners went into undertaking as it was a natural progression from making the coffins.

Nowadays, anyone can set up in the funeral business as most coffins now are brought in cheaply from abroad.

In 1949, I rented a workshop of my own in Banks Road, opposite the pumping station and set up as a wheelwright. There were still a lot of horses on the farms and, because of the War, not so many tractors and cars.

In 1953, I went back to undertaking at Harry Porter's whose workshop was in Cypress Road. I used to have to lay out the bodies and help with the pall-bearing and, at the cemetery, I'd place the green cloth at the sides of the grave for when they lowered the coffin. When the mourners gathered round, I'd be behind a headstone taking their names to give to the newspaper because, in those days, they published full details of funerals including everyone who attended.

I was at Porter's four years and then I moved to Bertie Wright's in Threlfall's Lane. We did mostly shop-fitting and alterations. Southport was a town full of small back-entry businesses and individual shops like Bates in the Cambridge Arcade who sold everything from haberdashery to carriagecandles for horse-drawn vehicles. The only really big firm was Brockhouses in Crossens who made Corgi scooters, which were dropped behind enemy lines by parachute in the War for the soldiers to ride.

In 1964, after a short spell at Frank Gatley's builders in Lydiate, Edward moved to Scarisbrick Estates where he stayed until the estate closed down in 1980.

Scarisbrick Estates owned a lot of the land in and around Southport. I worked in their Yard opposite the Plough. That went when they widened the dual carriageway a few years ago. When they closed down, I carried on the work with my son, Albert, fulfilling all their old contracts.

There aren't too many wheelwrights still around but then surely there can't be much work for them anymore can there? Horses and carts belong to history. And what is a bodger anyway?

Work? You'd be surprised. We never stop. As well as Albert, my other son, Alan, is in the trade and my daughter's 23-year-old son, Phil, works with me in the business as well.

A bodger is a man who operates a pole lathe and we're all members of the Association of Polelathe Turners and Greenwood Workers, There's over 500 members worldwide.

I trained my daughter Susan, Philip's mother, to do wheelwrighting but she married a man who breeds and looks after racing greyhounds so she has her hands full now with the dogs.

In the thirties and forties, when there were plenty of horse drawn vehicles, we made wheels for coal merchants, like Nicky Aughton in Banks, traders and milkmen. Farmers like Joe Houghton of Banks Road used horses and carts to deliver their own milk in jugs. It came straight from the cow, none of your pasteurised stuff then.

We still make wheels for shrimp carts although there's not as many today. We used to see a procession of them walking very slowly down the road on their way to the shore, just like a wagon train. They had to walk slowly so the horses wouldn't break into a sweat and then catch cold in the water.

As for the work, well for a start, we don't just do wheelwrighting. We make and repair benches, church pews, settles and seats. We have the contract to repair and varnish all the wooden benches and seats throughout Sefton for the council.

We do work for 'Lost Art', a company who specialise in recreating and restoring artefacts from a bygone age, like statues, fountains, carriages, gates, benches, etc. There is a lot of business to be had from the re-enactment societies that stage replicas of old battles, medieval jousts etc., They want things like wheels for canons. Then there is the restoration work in stately homes.

We make wheels for gypsy wagon, the carts on Liverpool wholesale fruit markets and those fancy stalls on wheels that you see standing in the Albert Dock and Wayfarers Arcade. And, of course, there are an awful lot of vintage and repro carriages and carts used in films and television that need repairing or replacing.

We regularly exhibit at heritage fairs, flower shows, agricultural shows and country fairs.

I came away from Edward's workshop quite amazed to have discovered that what I thought was a dying trade was thriving to such an extent in the 21st century and, also, very impressed with the skill needed.

As I left, Edward told me he is now teaching himself to make barrels and showed me a perfect model. He is 79. And they say you can't teach an old dog new tricks.

PROGRAMMES AND ADVERTS

Early SDC programme with list of members

Photo courtesy of Charles Preston

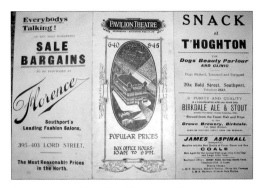

Programme for the Pavilion Theatre at the Pier Head

Photo courtesy of Charles Preston

Advert for Ben Purser's furniture shop, Lord St

Photo courtesy of Mike Swift

Ellis & Son's poster denoting Sale of Scala Theatre effects, 1962

Photo courtesy of Charles Preston

Left: Early Programme for the Garrick Theatre
Photo courtesy of Charles Preston

Right: An SDC Programme for a show at the Opera House, 1928
Photo courtesy of Jean Alexander

Cambridge Hall & Atkinson Library, Lord St, 1964

Birkdale Library, 2006

Librarian Erica Crabtree at Marshside Library in the Marshside Temperance Hall, Shellfield Rd, 1964

Churchtown Library, 1964

Crossens Library, 1964

The interior of Central Library, 1964 with Audrey Spencer, Betty Howard & Joyce Hall (Librarians)

LIBRARIES – Photos by Ron Ellis

Retirement of Marjorie Ackers and Barbara Ince - Librarians, Birkdale Library, 1975

Retirement of Chief Librarian Mr. B.T.W. Stevenson, 1964

Wayfares Shop in Leyland Arcarde

Photo courtesy of Arthur Pedlar

Leyland Arcade showing gallery where the band played

Photo courtesy of Arthur Pedlar

Palais de Danse, Lord St

Photo courtesy of Alan Pinch

Triocadero Cinema, Lord St

Photo courtesy of Alan Pinch

Haughton House, Circa 1913

Photo courtesy of Martin Connard

Demolition

Photo courtesy of Martin Connard

Wayfarers Arcade showing shops along
balcony and cafe area

Photo by Ron Ellis

Festival in Wayfarers Arcade featuring
local estate agent Ian Hitchcock

Photo by Ron Ellis

Woolworths 2006

Photo by Ron Ellis

Sainsburys 2006

Photo by Ron Ellis

Palladium Cinema. later the Gaumont
and then the Odeon

Photo courtesy of Martin Connard

Opening of the Palladium Cinema,
January, 1914

Photo courtesy of Martin Connard

BEFORE AND AFTER - SHERWOOD COTTAGE

Sherwood Cottage in Station Rd, once the home of Southport Swimming Champion
Margaret Howe (neé Tillot)

Photo courtesy of Margart Howe

...now replaced by a parade of shops called Sherwood House

Photo courtesy of Margaret Howe

BEFORE AND AFTER - BIRKDALE TOWN HALL

Birkdale Town Hall and Carnegie Library, 1964

New shops and offices in inferior architectural style

King George V Grammar School - Masons House, 1953

Norwood Road School, 1951

SCHOOLS

St Philip's C of E School, 1946. Teacher is Mrs. Plant, daughter of headmaster Cyril Rimmer

Winterdyne School, June 1947

Photo courtesy of Charles Preston

BEFORE AND AFTER - MASONIC BUILDINGS, LORD ST.

1889 - Built by Walter Connard

Photo courtesy of Martin Connard

2006

Photo courtesy of Ron Ellis

BEFORE AND AFTER (3)

Sally's Cottage at turn of the century

Alan Pinch outside the same cottage in 2006

PROGRAMME

Commencing MONDAY, 2nd September, 1957, at the Scala Theatre

The SOUTHPORT REPERTORY Co.

presents

"SPIDER'S WEB"

by AGATHA CHRISTIE

Characters : (in order of appearance).

Sir Rowland Delahaye	DONALD PELMEAR
Hugo Birch	VINT GRAVES
Jeremy Warrender	BRIAN DICKINSON
Clarissa Hailsham-Brown	JEAN ALEXANDER
Pippa Hailsham-Brown	SANDRA MARSH
Mildred Peake	EILEEN DERBYSHIRE
Elgin	STEPHEN THORNE
Oliver Costello	ARTHUR SPRECKLEY
Henry Hailsham-Brown	RONALD WILKINSON
Inspector Lord	PETER SCHOFIELD
Constable Jones	CHRISTOPHER DYER

PRODUCED by DONALD BODLEY

Setting painted by BERYL BUNN and SUSAN JOHNSON

We are greatly indebted to the following for Properties used in this Production

Gibson's, Chapel Street, and Staffordshire House, Lord Street, and Cristaloza, Cambridge Arcade, for China and Glassware.
Metcalfe's, Lord Street, and O. Bain, Eastbank Street, for Dressings.
Jay's, Cambridge Arcade, and Slaters, Chapel Street, for Cigarette Boxes.
Nylon Stockings by Kayser.   Table Lighter by Ronson.
Olivier Cigarettes, by Benson and Hedges.

• If you enjoy the Play, tell your friends •

The action takes place in the drawing-room of Copplestone Court, the Hailsham-Brown's home in Kent.

ACT I.
An evening in March.

INTERVAL

ACT II.
Scene 1. A quarter of an hour later.
Scene 2. Ten minutes later.

INTERVAL

ACT III.
A few minutes later.

PATRONS are reminded that COFFEE, ICE CREAM, SOFT DRINKS, etc., are on sale in the THEATRE FOYER during EACH INTERVAL.

Next Week

we present

THE RECENT DUCHESS THEATRE SUCCESS

"Plaintiff in a Pretty Hat"

A DELIGHTFUL WITTY COMEDY

by

HUGH and MARGARET WILLIAMS

BOOKING OFFICE OPEN 10 a.m. to 8 p.m. DAILY
YOU MAY ALSO BOOK BY TELEPHONE - 2426

Above: Cast of Agatha Christie's 'Spiders Web' performed in 1957
Below: Cast of Noel Coward's 'Relative Values' performed in 1953

Morning Coffee / Light Luncheons	★	FARMHOUSE CAFE BURTONS ARCADE (WHERE THE ORCHESTRA PLAYS)	★	Dainty Teas / Homely Comforts	FOYER DECORATION BY BOLTONS, *Florists* BIRKDALE, SOUTHPORT

Commencing MONDAY, 14th September, 1953, at the Little Theatre

THE SOUTHPORT REPERTORY COMPANY

presents

'RELATIVE VALUES'

A Light Comedy in Three Acts
by NOEL COWARD

Characters : (in order of their appearance)

Crestwell	TOM GOWLING
Alice	HILARY STRELITZ
Mrs. Moxton	MALQUITTA FERMO
Felicity, Countess of Marshwood	ELIZABETH McKENZIE
Lady Hayling	JEAN ALEXANDER
The Hon. Peter Ingleton	STANLEY LLOYD
Admiral Sir John Hayling	VINT GRAVES
Miranda Frayle	SHIRLEY CAMERON
The Earl of Marshwood	PETER MYERS
Don Lucas	ROGER OSTIME

The Play

PRODUCED by DONALD BODLEY

SETTINGS PAINTED by ARTHUR NUGENT

• If you enjoy the Play, tell your friends •

General Manager	J. HAROLD SMITH
Director of Productions	DONALD BODLEY
Stage Managers	NORMAN CUNNINGHAM STANLEY LLOYD
Assistant Stage Managers	HILARY STRELITZ ADRIENNE EVROLL
Electrician and Carpenter	ARTHUR NUGENT

The action of the play takes place in Marshwood House, East Kent.
Time:—The present.

ACT I.
SCENE 1. Saturday afternoon. After lunch.
SCENE 2. A few hours later.

INTERVAL

ACT II.
SCENE 1. Before dinner.
SCENE 2. After dinner.

INTERVAL

ACT III.
The next morning.

PATRONS are reminded that COFFEE, ICE CREAM, SOFT DRINKS, etc., are on sale in the THEATRE FOYER during EACH INTERVAL.

DEAR PATRONS,
Next week we present our last play of our 1953 season at the Little Theatre and we have chosen a riotous comedy, "My Sister Eileen." Some years ago it was an outstanding success as a film. I am sure you will find it more outstanding as a play.

The week after we finish here, we commence a new season at the Scala Theatre. We recommend that you reserve your permanent seats now.

Yours sincerely, DONALD BODLEY.

YOU MAY BOOK BY TELEPHONE - 3021

ACKNOWLEDGMENTS.
Furniture by Blackburn's, Upper Aughton Road.
Electrical Fittings by Grahame Brown, Eastbank Street.
Antiques, Ornaments etc., by Hague's, Tulketh St., and Bain's, Eastbank St.
Pictures by Giddens, London Street, and Greaves, 18 Ashley Road.
China and Glassware by Gibson's, Chapel St., and R. A. Jacob, Tulketh St.
Carpets by Swift's, Eastbank Street Bridge.
Silverware by Jacquies, Lord Street.
Other Properties kindly loaned by the Doll's Hospital, Princes Street.
Furs by M. Fletcher, (Master Furrier,) Lord Street.
Nylon Stockings by Kayser Bondor.

The Public may leave at the end of the Performance by all exits, and all exit doors must at that time be open.

If the Public leave in an orderly manner THIS THEATRE CAN BE EMPTIED IN THREE MINUTES OR LESS.

AT THE SCALA THEATRE - All Photos courtesy of Jean Alexander

- For all things Musical -

PIANOS : RADIOGRAMS
RADIO : TELEVISION
RECORD PLAYERS
SHEET MUSIC
RECORDS

Phone:
56972
(3 Lines)

ALDRIDGES
(Music) Limited

Open
All Day
Saturdays

14-16 HOGHTON ST., SOUTHPORT

SCALA THEATRE, (Kingsway,) SOUTHPORT
Licensee: W. PEEL SMITH

The Public may leave at the end of the performance by all exits,
and all exit doors must at that time be open.

The fireproof curtain shall at all times be maintained in working
order and shall be lowered at the beginning of and during the
time of every performance.

If the Public leave in an orderly manner, THIS THEATRE CAN
BE EMPTIED IN THREE MINUTES OR LESS.

Irene's
The Little Shop for the Fuller Figure
GOWNS, COATS, SUITS, and UNDERWEAR
We Specialise in O.S. and X.O.S.

Announcing a Special Service for the Elderly & Infirm

Infirm and Elderly Ladies are invited to ring
Southport 56597 for selection of Gowns
in their own Home.

4 UNION STREET, (Lord Street,) SOUTHPORT
Tel.: SOUTHPORT 56597

The Bookshop of Quality & Note

C. K. Broadhurst & Co.
For RARE BOOKS, FIRST EDITIONS
and ALL NEW BOOKS
5 & 7 Market Street, Southport
LIBRARIES PURCHASED

Phone 2064   *(Just off Lord Street)*

Madge Brewer, Ltd.
CONFECTIONERS

Specialities: WEDDING CAKES, BIRTHDAY CAKES, ANNIVERSARY CAKES

14 CHAPEL STREET – Tel. 5253   98 BOTANIC ROAD, CHURCHTOWN—Tel. 88334
17-19 EASTBANK ST.—Tel. 5253   122 STATION ROAD, AINSDALE—Tel. 77105

... Southport ...

SOUTHPORT REPERTORY COMPANY LTD.

General Manager	J. HAROLD SMITH
Stage Director	PETER CLAYTON
Stage Manager	DEREK BANCROFT
Assistant Stage Managers	CHRISTOPHER DYER, SANDRA MARSH
	JOHN LOUKES, MOIRA COLLIN
Stage Carpenter	EDWARD HEDGES
Electrician	EDWARD CANNELL

Director of Productions	DONALD BODLEY

BOX OFFICE OPEN 10-0 a.m. to 8-0 p.m.   Telephone 2426

WILKINSON'S
(THE GIFT CORNER)

10 CORONATION WALK · · SOUTHPORT

:: **Gifts for All Occasions** ::

JEWELLERY :: TOYS :: FANCY GOODS, Etc.
AGENT FOR DINKY TOYS

Adverts from the programmes showing contemporary local businesses of the 1950's

---

THE SOUTHPORT REPERTORY COMPANY
TOURING in JANUARY

Grand Opening Production of
SPRING SEASON
AT
THE CASINO THEATRE
MONDAY, FEBRUARY 2ND.
1953

BOOKING PLANS FOR THE FIRST PRODUCTION AT
THE BOX OFFICE, LITTLE THEATRE

AT THE LITTLE THEATRE
THE
SOUTHPORT DRAMATIC CLUB
will present
"A Play for Ronnie"
A play in Three Acts by Warren Chetham Strode
Produced by DUDLEY S. WOLF

FRIDAY, JANUARY 23TH, 1953
for EIGHT NIGHTS at 7-45 p.m.

BOX OFFICE OPENS at 11-0 a.m. on Monday 19th January

RIMMER & WILDE, Printers, 109A Eastbank Street, SOUTHPORT. Tel.: 4815.

On Monday, 18th January, 1954
The Southport Repertory Company
present
HERE AT THE SCALA THEATRE
A NEW SEASON
OF FAMOUS PLAYS

Watch for Announcement of our
Grand Opening Production

**TOYS on X'MAS TREE are "RODDY TOYS," kindly given by
D. G. Todd & Co. Ltd., makers of "Roddy Toys."
These will be given to the Children's Hospital in the New Year.**

The Southport Musical Society
(Affiliated to the National Operatic & Dramatic Association)
present
FOR ONE WEEK ONLY
"THE ARCADIANS"
Book by MARK AMBRENT
Music by LIONEL MONKTON & HOWARD TALBOT
AT THE SCALA THEATRE
Commencing Monday, 11th January, 1954
Nightly at 7-30 p.m.

TICKETS, 2.6 to 5/-   Saturday Evening, 3/- to 6.6
BOOKING OFFICE NOW OPEN

RIMMER & WILDE, Printers, 109A Eastbank Street, SOUTHPORT. Tel.: 4815.

SOUTHPORT F.C. - Photos courtesy of Ron Ellis

Above: Manager Liam Watson with his Nationwide Conference North Championship winning squad 2004-5

Below:Southport fans celebrate the club's appearance at Wembley for the F.A. Trophy Final, 1998.

SOUTHPORT F.C. - Photos courtesy of Ron Ellis

Above: The 'Trust in Yellow' Supports Trust - Jon O'Byrne (Trust in Yellow); Paul Cook (SFC Manager); Rob Urwin (Trust in Yellow); 2006

Left: Botanic Gardens Museum Exhibition 2003 - Celebrating 125 years of Southport FC (1881-2006); organised by Mike Braham & Geoff Wilde

Below; Eileen & Harry Howard with Southport fans inside Wembley Stadium for F.A. Trophy Final v Cheltenham Town, 1998. Southport lost 1-0.

MOMENTS OF HISTORY

Showjumping at Southport Flower Show
on Victoria Park
                    Photo courtesy of Marie Murray

Lord Ronnie Fearn with Lib Dem Leader
Charles Kennedy and Mike Braham
successfully campaigning to save the
Magistrates Court, circa 2000
                    Photo courtesy of Mike Braham

One of the first cars in Southport at 1
Lulworth Road
                    Photo courtesy of Charles Preston

The Old Ainsdale Lido circa 1940.
Became the Ainsdale Discovery Centre
in 1999, part of Sefton Coast
Partnership
                    Photo courtesy of David Harrision

A Tiger Moth plane in Hesketh Drive
aircraft hangor
                    Photo courtesy of Phil King

Steam locomotive on the Lakeside
Minature Railway

STEVE DICKSON

Steve Dickson was the instigator of Southport's first radio station, Dune FM. He was born at Park House, Waterloo on Dec 9th 1959. The family moved to Formby when he was 6 months old and he attended St Luke's School and Formby High School.

My introduction to Steve came when he invited me to become one of the first presenters on the embryonic radio station that was to become Dune FM.

However, when I interviewed him for this book at his Ainsdale home in February 2006, he had moved on. He was now the Chief Executive of the Sefton Chamber of Commerce. He stressed to me that he had always pursued a business, as opposed to a show business, career.

I started the radio station as a commercial venture. Since leaving school after A-levels, I had worked in retail management with Debenhams; was a salesman then area sales manager for Tetrosyl (industrial chemicals, paint and DIY); was one of two national sales trainers then national accounts manager and worked in Africa for Rothmans International. Finally, prior to the successful Dune FM licence victory in 1997,I worked for U.S. conglomerate, Tenneco, which took me into Europe and speaking at conferences in Africa and Singapore. That was twenty years of business training and experience.

Throughout this time, Steve had been involved with broadcasting. It all started when he was just 14.

From 1967 to 1974, my father, Norman, managed the Somewhere Else club in Neville Street. It had one of the first sound-to-light psychedelic dance floors in the North West. As a young lad, I used to help him stock the bar with the Babychams, Cherry B's, Watney's Red Barrel, Double Diamond and Newcastle Brown ales. I also help scrape the chewing gum off the dance floor!

Sometimes, the DJ's would leave their equipment behind for the next night and I would practice working the decks. At performed my first gig at 14. When Tommy Barton and Tony Stannard bought the club and re-named it The Dandy, I applied for the DJ's job. At first I was turned down but I spent £50 having a jingle made incorporating the club's name and they hired me for a Monday and Tuesday night for £15.

I started in hospital radio in 1980 at Southport alongside Peter Smee, Phil Hilton and Paul Welles (Derrick Shatwell). The station was funded entirely by charitable donations. The hospital trust merely provided the space to operate.

Around 1987, I moved into station management at Ormskirk Hospital, which very soon had to be relocated due to the new hospital site being expanded. With two colleagues we negotiated long and hard with the hospital management and had state of the art studios built for us to my design.

In 1991, the Radio Authority announced the launching of Restricted Service Licences for local radio stations serving an area not properly covered by existing stations. Phil Hilton was now with BBC Radio Merseyside and he suggested to Steve that they should try for a licence for Southport.

I asked him, 'what are the odds of us succeeding?' I wasn't an anorak; I was a businessman. Phil said the chances were good. I devised a business plan and we decided we should give it a go. Phil could provide the broadcasting resources and I'd handle the advertising and finance side.

We paid £1 each for an off-the- shelf limited company and applied for a 28 day RSL licence. We broadcast from a caravan parked behind Southport Theatre that we hired from a Warrington radio station called WFMR, who later became Wyre FM. Our aim was to provide a mixture of music and speech featuring local news and sport. Our income came from advertising so I set up a sales team and went out myself bringing in business.

My role at Dune FM was football reporter on Southport FC with commentary from the home matches at Haig Avenue. I also did an hour-long 'nostalgia' programme, interviewing local personalities to talk about their lives in Southport. A bit like this book, really, except that on the show they got to choose a favourite piece of music as well.

George Sephton (the 'Voice of Anfield)', John Cooper and Chris Mills were among the other broadcasters on that first trial. John only left Dune in 2006. He was the last one of the original team. We put up Day-Glo posters along the coast road advertising 100.6 Dune FM., our original spot on the dial. We lost £700 at the end of the month but the concept of local radio was well received and we went on to do three more trial runs before we put in for the permanent licence.

When Steve made his application to the Radio Authority for Dune FM, it was the area that was granted the licence, not the station. Incredibly, once Southport was deemed to be suitable for a radio station of its own, anyone was allowed to tender for the licence, even though Dune FM had done all the groundwork. Steve accepted this with equanimity.

Not every station that had applied in other towns won the licence either, but that was because they were perhaps not as efficient as others that applied, or their business plan didn't stand up. After all, we ourselves were a bunch of amateurs in that we'd never run a radio station before and we found ourselves up against professionals. It wasn't a foregone conclusion we'd win.

Two people put up against Dune FM for the Southport licence, both experienced companies who already owned existing stations.

Godfrey Williams' Marcher Sound had three radio stations already and they put forward an application for Diamond FM. Our other competitor was Peter Salt's Independent Radio Group who had Wish FM and three other stations. His proposed station was called Mere FM. Both of them tried to persuade me at different times to go in with them but it meant I would not have total control so I wasn't interested. Each of them told me I was being silly, as I'd no chance against them.

I felt we needed somebody with managerial experience in commercial radio to assist the application and help secure the win I recruited David Maker to come in as chairman. He had started Jazz FM, following success with Red Rose Radio group. The total investment from a mix of shareholders was £236,000. I was only in this for the win. I didn't want to be second. We won the licence on April 10th 1997 after a three-month delay by the radio authority evaluating the submissions. It was a momentous day when we got that phone call from London.

Just nine months on from the launch, we had a 13% audience reach with 26,000 listeners a week. (Figures from Radio Joint Audience Research Limited). Interestingly, Dune FM in 2005 had only a 12% reach, so we must have done something right.

In July 1998, we ran a secondary service called Golf FM to support the British Open Golf Championship at Royal Birkdale and, in the same year, we broadcast live from Wembley Stadium when Southport FC played Cheltenham Town in the F.A. Trophy final. I co-hosted the programme in the studio down an ISDN line with Ron Ellis and Ray O'Brien commentating on the match, which Southport sadly lost 1-0.

Steve left Dune FM in 1999 with the station being sold to Kenny James and his new Forward Media group. David Maker rolled in part of his shareholding into the new company. In 2004, current owners, The Local Radio Company who already owned 24 local radio stations, took over.

As a business exercise, it worked well. All the shareholders made money and we developed a strong brand radio station. Phil Hilton still works in radio for the BBC. [I moved on to the next venture.]

The next venture for Steve was forming his own marketing business, The Development Company, based on the Promenade. He grew a client base supplying marketing and advertising strategies for small to medium businesses.

In 2000 he joined the board of Sefton Chamber of Commerce and helped develop the first Prestige Ball and Sefton Business Awards, held at the Floral Hall in October 2002, when his company also designed and delivered the audio-visual on the night.

Formby impresario, Paul Stone, put on the entertainment when we had the annual Sefton Business Awards. In 2006, I moved the date to February, which was a good move as it didn't clash with pre-Christmas events like the Ambassadors Awards and instead became the first black tie function of the New Year. Remember, the Chamber's only income is from subscriptions, lunches, raffles and events like this. 410 people turned up last Friday and we made £8,500 profit. I set up a screen on the stage and showed pictures of Southport in Queensland, Australia and had a live phone link with the chairman of their Chamber of Commerce in which we announced a raffle with a prize of a trip for two people to visit each other's town. The reaction was tremendous.

Steve is also on the board of the Southport Flower Show as a trustee director in which role he oversees marketing strategy.

The show has developed over the years into far more of an entertainment and educational experience rather than a purist horticultural only show. It is building in stature and I'm very proud of its ongoing success.

I actually preferred the show when it featured show jumping and sheepdog trials but didn't say so. Instead I wondered what Steve's next venture would be as I was certain there would be many more different fields left that he would want to conquer.

PETER EATON

Peter Eaton owns June The Florists, one of Southport's oldest businesses which was first opened in the 1920's by his grandmother, Bessie Eaton. He was born at St. Katherine's Maternity Home in February 1960

Strangely, I had never met Peter before I visited him at his home in July 2006. I say strangely because he knew just about everybody in the book yet our paths had never crossed.

I went to Kew Preparatory School when I was just two years old. At four, I moved to Notre Dame Convent, which stood at the corner of Weld Road and Lulworth Road. We were taught by the nuns and there were only seven or eight boys there, the rest were girls. I was the last boy to leave. The main subjects were Maths, English and Playtime, no history or geography or anything like that.

From 1966 to 1976, I attended Scarisbrick Hall School where the Headmaster was Mr. Oxley. It had only been opened for about three years and most of the pupils at that time were boarders who came from all over the world. The coach collected me from Southport every morning.

Mr. Oxley was a wonderful man and they gave me an excellent education but I left at sixteen to join the family business.

So tell me about the family business, as there can't be many people in Southport who have never shopped at June The Florist.

It was founded by my grandmother, Bessie Eaton, who started by selling flowers from a handcart round Hesketh Park way back in the early 1920's. Often she would keep back a couple of stems from every dozen and give them away to people who were unable to afford them. She later became Mayoress in 1969-70.

Bessie's first shop was in the basement of Westminster Chambers in Lord Street, just along the road from the Palace Cinema. It was here where she started with my grandfather, Victor. They soon moved premises to the corner of Eastbank Street and Lord Street where it still is today.

The shop was named after their daughter, June, the intention being to open a second shop named after their son, Jack, my father.

My father and mother took over the running of the shop when Bessie retired and, a few years later, I came on board and we opened a second shop in Birkdale Village. We decided to keep the name June as it was already established and had a good reputation.

After that we kept on expanding until we had twelve shops, including Formby, Ainsdale, Ormskirk and Hillside.

Today, the retail side of the business is supported in terms of revenue by the Internet. We have eight Internet websites, which are open, of course, twenty-four hours a day. We have a strong telesales team and there is also Interflora which is always very popular.

Most of our stock is brought over from Holland in refrigerated trucks and we have approximately four deliveries a week.

We won the 'Best in Show' prize at the Southport Flower Show six years running and now feel we do not need to enter. It used to be such a grand event when they had showjumping with riders like Harvey Smith and David Broome competing.

The most popular flowers today are roses, lilies and orchids, compared to years ago when carnations and chrysanthemums were favoured. Most of our stock is now available all the year round with only a few varieties being seasonal.

But it isn't just flowers that June's deal in.

In 1987, when my wife, Elizabeth joined the business, we were one of the first people in the country to open a balloon decoration shop. Now they are all over the country. We also hire linen chair covers for weddings, parties, functions, etc. Decoration and high profile flower arrangements are a large part of the business and we travel all over the country. The corporate side of the business is also very strong.

We are now the largest florist of our kind in the North West and have a great team of staff, not forgetting our three children Peter, Georgina and Emily who all help, particularly with the large functions.

Although Lord Street is still our flagship store, most of our business is done from our King Street head offices where Roy Lloyd Motor Body Repair shop used to be before he moved to Hall Street Business Centre..

There are not many family businesses left on Lord Street and our goal is customer satisfaction. Weddings and funerals are a very important part of our business, be they church services or civil ceremonies with receptions, and can be complemented by the different ways we can decorate each event.

In the 1970's there would be queues along the road outside our shop at eight on a Saturday morning and we would have completely sold out of everything by late afternoon.

Pay and display and, now, pedestrianisation have ripped the heart out of the town. People don't want to come to somewhere where they have to queue to park then pay for the privilege when they can go elsewhere and park free of charge. Plus the fact that there are so many supermarkets in and around the town with free parking making the individual shopkeeper almost redundant! Trade is not so easy with all these obstacles..

Apart from floristry, I asked Peter about his social life in the town.

When I was young, the place to go was El Tonel Wine Bar in West Street owned by John Cohen, which late became The Glasshouse. It was the first wine bar in Southport and it was a wonderful place to meet the local characters. These days, Elizabeth and I like to go to The Warehouse Brasserie, the Auberge, Owens Restaurant and Crystals.

I have been involved in many sports in the town. I played tennis for the Argyle Tennis Club and a lot of my social life there was centred around there. I played football for Southport Amateurs and Southport Trinity and badminton for Southbank Road Badminton Club. I swam at Victoria Baths and represented Southport at swimming. I spent time water-skiing on the Marine Lake and played table tennis at the Drill Hall behind the YMCA in Manchester Road.

The Drill Hall was demolished just a few weeks before I interviewed Peter, and yet another large apartment block stands in its place.

My son, Peter, attended Sandhurst Military Academy and is one of the youngest officers in the British Army and my sisters, Judy and Lisa, are both show jumpers who have ridden at Hickstead and Wembley. They kept their horses in stables behind our houses in Lord Street West. So, you see, we are a very active family. My daughters Georgina and Emily play hockey, tennis and swimming.

So what is the future for June's the Florists?

We have a new project which we are developing at the moment which is a totally new concept with flowers. Something completely different that will be launched shortly in Liverpool.

Before I met Peter, I had not realised what big business floristry had become. My daughter, Nikki, is attending a floristry course in Sydney, where she lives, so I can perhaps look forward to her keeping me in grand style in my old age.

GEOFFREY ELLIS

Geoffrey Ellis ran the Christian Book Centre in Wesley Street for 36 years. He was born at the White Heather Nursing Home in Southport on October 13th 1937 and has spent most of his life in the town.

Geoffrey is one of those people you see so often around the town that you eventually say hello because you feel you must know him. And there can be few local residents who have not visited, at one time of another, one of the longest established shops in Southport.

I spent a pleasant afternoon with Geoffrey at his modern Marshside bungalow and learnt more about the history of Southport churches than any vicar could have told me.

The following weekend, his book 'Dissenters of All Persuasions' was to be launched so my interview was like a preview. Luckily, I'd already ordered and paid for my copy.

My grandfather was a builder. He built many of the houses around Bakers Lane and Cambridge Avenue. We lived at 43 Baker's Lane which was half of the first pair of houses built between Marshside Road and Cambridge Road.

My first school was Emmanuel Primary, now replaced by flats, which I attended between the ages of five and eight before going on to Churchtown and KGV. I left the classroom at KGV at 16 to go and work in the school office along with Miss Craig who had been secretary at the original building at Woodlands. The caretaker at the time was Arthur Wilkinson.

The headmaster, Geoffrey Dixon was fresh from Sandhurst and very keen on discipline. A heinous offence, such as giving cheek to a prefect, merited the cane. One of my duties as office boy was to hand him a bamboo cane from a stock of in the corner of his office and stay to witness the beating. Four or six strokes were applied, depending on the severity of the offence, and as the boy straightened up, usually in tears, the headmaster would dismiss him with the instruction, 'get yourself together'.

Although the school was part of Southport Corporation Education Dept, certain of our accounts such as uniforms, dinner money and kitchen expenses were controlled internally and came under my jurisdiction.

After spending two years in the RAF doing his National Service between 1955 and 1957, Geoffrey took an admin job at English Tools in Wigan. After five years there, he moved to the Midlands to be a sales rep for the company but returned to Southport to stay in 1965 when he bought the Christian Book Shop from Keith Lee who had started the business in Stanley Street before moving to premises at 3 Wesley Street.

When I moved in, paperbacks were one and three-pence and there were few religious books published. The only other shop selling similar material was a Catholic repository in Eastbank Street but they also sold 'Health and Efficiency' under the counter.

My family advised me against taking the shop but I knew I could make a success of it and I did so, despite the fact that, in recent years, many Christian bookshops have closed down due to rising rents and rates plus the closure of so many churches.

I decided it was not enough to wait for the customers to come into my shop. I had to go out and find them and take the product to them. It was a policy that worked well as we now have 50 bookstalls in churches all over Merseyside.

Today, there is a far greater quantity of religious literature published, of all kinds, together with videos, CD's, DVD's and other items that we call 'Holy Hardware'.

So which church has Geoffrey as a member of its congregation?

I was based at Christ Church on Lord Street from the age of ten until 1996 when many of the congregation left to join other churches. I was a churchwarden and still am a Patron of the Living, a committee that elects the new vicar.

Christ Church was always heavily involved with youth work. In the 60's and 70's we had over 150 kids in every Sunday night, we had 60 attending Bible study on a Tuesday and Saturday Recreation Night attracted a hundred or so, without any pop music.

However, for the last ten years, I have been worshipping at St. John's Church in Birkdale and I play the dame (badly) in their Christmas pantomime.

For 35 years from 1960, I ran a holiday camp at Polzeath in Cornwall. We had a staff of 35 to look after 110 kids for a fortnight. Nobody will run them any more. Like so many things nowadays, too much red tape.

I asked Geoffrey about the state of churches in Southport in 2006.

Well, like everywhere, church congregations have declined and many churches have closed. Evensong has virtually vanished as many older people are afraid to go out at nights. And there are more lay readers today than there are clergy with many ministers looking after two or three churches in a parish.

Southport still has a thriving number of churches, though, for its size. About sixty at the last count. There is a good Christian community in the town but the largest congregations are not always at the traditional churches. There are more independent churches opening as the old Methodist and Anglican ones close.

The Community Church in Southbank Road Road, in the old Southbank Road Methodist building, is very well attended. It's what is called a charismatic church. Christ Church still attracts a similar number as does the Elim Pentecostal in Manchester Road, another church described by some as 'happy-clappy'. Then there are other new churches like The Vineyard at KGV College, the Assembly of God Church, near the new ASDA store, and the Living Faith Fellowship whilst, at the other end of the spectrum, the Grace Baptist is still going strong in Princes Street. That is a very traditional church; in fact they used to be called the Strict and Particular Baptists.

The only church in Southport still using the old King James Bible is the Boundary Street Mission. The Drummersdale Mission near Bescar, out on Martin Mere, is affiliated to it and the 'pews' at Drummersdale are seats taken from Lord Street's old Trocadero Cinema.

The Jewish church has fared badly in Southport with many Jewish people moving back to Manchester. After the War, the Arnside Road Synagogue had as many as 1300 worshippers but now they are down to a tiny fraction of that and I believe the building is up for sale.

Although he sold his shop in 2005, Geoffrey is still involved in church activity.

I was a good friend of Charles Oxley, the one-time principal of Scarisbrick College. Together, we launched a campaign to oppose the opening of a local sex shop. 1300 people attended the meeting in the Floral Hall and the shop closed down after a few weeks. Sex shops have now smartened their image but they are still SEX SHOPS.

I am chairman of a national organisation called 'Key Change' which started out over a hundred years ago to provide clubs for girls in service in seaside resorts. Nowadays, they are drop-in centres for homeless women. We also have eleven retirement homes across the country.

I went to Geoffrey's book launch the following Saturday. It was held at the Baptist Church in Scarisbrick New Road (formerly known as the Onion Church before they dismantled the mosque-like roof). Tea and biscuits were served and the event was extremely well-attended. I am pleased to say 'Dissenters of all Persuasions' is a fascinating read and an extremely well produced, glossy book with lots of colour photos which I can recommend to everyone interested in the history of the town.

RON ELLIS

Ron Ellis was born at the Christiana Hartley Maternity Hospital on Sept 12th 1941 and has lived in Southport all his life. In 1992, The Sun newspaper hailed him as 'the man with the most jobs in Britain'.

He currently lives in Freshfield with his wife, Sue. They have two daughters and one grandchild.

Ron's parents met in the 1930's at a whist drive, one of the town's most popular social activities in that decade. His father worked at Brockhouses in Crossens as an engineer.

We lived in St. Luke's Grove, in a 3-bedroom house with an outside lavatory, at a weekly rent of 13/3d. (66p).

When I was 12 my mother and I moved in with her sisters who ran a grocers and confectioners shop (E. & M. Sherlock) at 25 Forest Road for 36 years. Customers used to bring in their orders on their way to St. Luke's Station, where they caught the 8.33am express to their work in Manchester, and collect them in the evening on the way home.

All the cakes and pies were baked in large gas ovens in the cellar next to the washhouse, which boasted a dolly tub and iron clothes mangle. There was no electricity on the premises. Lighting was by gas mantles although the kitchen and bathroom had only wall spigots. Heating was by coal fires. When the other kids at school watched the Coronation and The Grove Family on TV in the fifties, I listened to a wireless attached to an acid filled accumulator. Televisions didn't run on gas.

Ron went to St. Philip's School until he was eleven. Cyril Rimmer was the headmaster and his daughter, Mrs. Plant, was the infant teacher.

If you passed the 11-plus you went to KGV, which I did, but I was disappointed because, unlike the alternatives of Meols Cop and Christ Church, at KGV they played rugby and I wanted to play football.

I left KGV at 17 with 6 'O' levels. The careers master was a Mr. L.C. Hargreaves. I told him I wanted to be a reporter and I'd already taught myself shorthand and typing, but he said I was too quiet and shy and I'd be better off in a bookshop. His friend from the Rotary Club, Charlie Birkin, was the manager of W.H. Smiths. He'd have a word with him. The following week I was working at their shop at 479-81 Lord Street in the book department. That's how jobs were filled then. The manager was on £1000 a year, not a bad salary when £5000 would buy a house in Westbourne Road. I earned £6 a week.

Ron lasted four years at Smiths ending up as Assistant Manager and, more significantly, in charge of their circulating library, a rival to the one in the Lord Street branch of Boots. By the mid-sixties, both Boots and Smiths had closed them all down. In 1963, Ron joined Southport Public Library.

It was a great job. I was the only man amongst 33 women. I worked in all the branch libraries including Crossens and Wennington Road, both now shut down. The central Reference Librarian, Mrs.Latham, was housed in a glass-fronted cage whilst Wennington Road branch had a revolving counter that the junior staff used to ride on when no borrowers were about. At Churchtown, the first task of the librarian, Miss Bedford, was to stoke up the coke-filled boiler for the central heating. Southport Corporation paid me my full salary to go on the two year A.L.A. course at the Liverpool School of Librarianship.

Meanwhile, Ron had become involved with the Merseybeat craze that was sweeping the region at the start of the sixties with many local teenagers like Barry Womersley, Ray Marshall, Pete James and Kingsize Taylor all forming beat groups.

From the age of 15, I was very into American rock'n'roll music. I had a huge record collection and went to all the local youth clubs and venues like The Klic Klic and Glenpark Clubs where the Merseybeat groups were playing. I'd go backstage at the Liverpool Empire with my Brownie box camera, interview the stars and write reviews for the NME, Disc and Record Mirror.

I wanted to be in a group myself but I couldn't sing or play an instrument. One evening I was taking publicity photos at St Stephens Church Hall, Hightown for a Southport group called The Rave-Ons and they asked me to become their manager. I went round pubs and clubs asking for bookings and the first one I got for them was at The Ship Inn at Haskayne for a fee of £5 of which I got 10% - ten shillings (50p.). I was lucky; The Rave-Ons were a good band and people asked me if I had any more like them on my books. In no time I was running an agency.

Ron soon realised there was another route to the spotlight other than being in a group. He became a disc jockey.

I bought a pair of turntables, an amplifier, microphone and speakers and went on the road as a mobile DJ, one of the first in the North West. Between 1967 and 1987, I played in practically every hotel, golf club, social club, nightclub, golf club and dance hall in Southport. All in all, I did 2556 gigs in 40 years, the last one in 2005. Until 1976 and 'Saturday Night Fever', there were few D.J.'s on the road.

In 1968, having taken his library exams, Ron joined Lancashire County Libraries in charge of three Liverpool branch libraries but the bosses weren't happy when they found he was running a business and gave him an ultimatum – his career in the library or 'this silly pop music business'.

There was no choice. I was making more money, and having more fun, with the music. I got a job, instead, as a sales rep with Hall Bros. selling Mentholyptus cough sweets in Lancashire and Westmorland. Suddenly my groups started getting gigs in places like Carlisle and Blackburn and I toured the Lakes with the disco gear crammed next to the cough sweets in the company estate car.

Until Dec 1969, that is, when Halls invited him to choose between a promising career in sales or 'that silly pop music business'. Guess which he chose.

From New Years Day 1970 I was a self-employed DJ, Agent and Photographer (Wedding photos and publicity shots). I also joined Equity and appeared regularly on 'Coronation Street', 'Brookside', etc as an extra.

Thinking that being a DJ wouldn't last forever, Ron started buying up large Victorian houses and converted them into flats to rent out.

My first house was in Manchester Road. I paid £2,750. I got a £2500 mortgage from the Hastings & Thanet Building Society and borrowed the £250 deposit from a Liverpool moneylender who charged me a £52 'introductory fee' as well as the interest.

My mother and I lived on the ground floor and I converted upstairs into four bedsits let to nurses for £5 a week each. I then bought a house round the corner in Hawkshead Street, which was in six bedsits and a flat, for £3000. The vendor gave me a 50% private mortgage and the bank lent me the other half. Suddenly, I had eleven tenants all paying off the mortgages until, one day, both houses would be mine.

In 1970, there was little rented accommodation, and certainly no letting agents, so there was a huge demand for rented property. The only drawback was the Rent Officer. Tenants could sign up to pay an agreed rent then, once ensconced, apply for it to be reduced and there was nothing the landlord could do about it. Luckily, most people honoured their contracts.

Furnishings were very basic in 1970 compared with today. Kitchens had cabinets with pull out enamel worktops rather than fitted units and hot water came from Ascot heaters fitted over the sink. Beds had to be bolted together;

furniture and carpets were second-hand; rooms were heated by gas or electric fires with coin slot meters.

I went on to buy houses in Victoria Street, Lathom Road, The Promenade, Part Street and Duke Street, all in multi-occupation.

When Mrs Thatcher introduced poll tax, which later became council tax, landlords were in clover as the burden of paying the rates was switched from landlord to tenant. Standards were rising as tenants expected showers, fitted kitchens and wardrobes, central heating, washing machines and fitted carpets.

But back to the music.

By 1972, I was doing over 200 disco gigs a year, travelling round the country in my Mini Countryman, I made regular trips to record companies in London, cadging promo copies of new records, and in 1976, Warner Brothers offered me the job of Northern Promotions Manager.

I worked for Warner Brothers for two years, calling at discotheques and clubs from Birmingham to Scotland, promoting the latest records. In 1978, I set up my own company, Northern Disco Promotion Services, and arranged promotion tours for visiting pop stars like Mary Stavin (Miss World) and Viola Wills. I booked the hotels, radio station interviews and disco appearances in advance then drove them round the country myself. When we were appearing near Southport, I booked them into the Bold Hotel as I was resident DJ there at the time.

Also in 1978, Ron married Sue and decided to take a 'real job' to support his new wife and their two young daughters.

I was the U.K. sales rep for Claude Gill Books for two years, selling magazine subscriptions to libraries all over Britain. I fitted the record promoting round the day job and came home at weekends to do my disco gigs.

He also found time to write his first crime novel and make a record.

'Murder First Glass' was published by Robert Hale who gave me £100 for it. Not much considering I was being paid £75 a time for magazine articles at the time.

I'd written several songs and made a couple of records in the early 70's, hiring top session men to back me. When punk rock came out in 1979, I wrote a number called 'Boys on the Dole' which I recorded under the name of Neville Wanker & The Punters. I sold it to Lightning Records for £1000 and it reached No 7 in the New Wave charts. Sixties star, P.J. Proby, recorded two of my songs in 1989.

In 1983, Ron joined international Tax & Business Law publishers, CCH Editions Ltd., as Area Sales Manager, calling on accountants and solicitors in the North West. It was a job he held for 13 years until the company was taken over by a Dutch company in 1996 and the 48-strong sales force was disastrously replaced by two telesales girls.

I still carried on doing the disco, buying more houses, writing magazine articles and book and CD review and taking the odd TV part.

In 1989, I opened a teashop. I looked at the Fleur de Lys Café at the corner of Lord Street and Portland Street, opposite the Price of Wales Hotel, but the rent was £12k pa, the rates £12k pa and they wanted £20k ingoing. I couldn't see it paying off.

Instead, I paid £17k for the freehold of a derelict newsagent's shop in Shakespeare Street and turned it into an old-fashioned teashop with a flat above. We served Darjeeling tea in China cups banned smoking, displayed copies of Country Life and played classical CD's in the background. Sue made the food, mostly vegetarian, and we called the cafe Small Talk. Popular Radio Merseyside presenters, Billy Butler and Wally Scott, performed the opening ceremony but the venture only lasted six months by which time I'd lost £5,600. People wanted bacon butties, the Daily Mirror, ciggies and Madonna. Not Vivaldi.

Also in 1989, I wrote a book called 'Journal of a Coffin Dodger', an Adrian Mole-type diary about a man of 84 who decides to become a playboy. I had 26 rejections from publishers so I had I printed it myself and sold over 5000 copies. I was Chairman of Southport Writers Circle at the time.

I was one of the original presenters at Southport's first radio station, Dune FM. I hosted a 'Southport nostalgia' programme talking to local residents and playing music from their era. When Southport reached the F.A. Trophy final, I did the full match commentary from Wembley Stadium, assisted by Ray O'Brien.

When Ron left CCH in 1996, he decided to become a full time writer.

I say full-time. By then I had 60 flats in Southport but I sold them all and invested the proceeds in property in London's Docklands. Less hassle. In Southport, 85% of the tenants were on housing benefit, the council were way behind with payments and the class of tenants had deteriorated alarmingly since the seventies.

I had also become the Southport F.C. correspondent for the Southport Champion, having been a supporter of the club since 1947. I was the P.A. announcer there for several years in the 60's and 70's and older supporters still remember the players running out to my signature tune (The Crystals' 'Da Doo Ron Ron') over the Tannoy.

For a couple of years I ran a course for Liverpool University on the History of Popular Music 1930-80. The classes were held at Holy Trinity Church Hall in Hoghton Street.

I play from time to time in the Southport & Formby Quiz League for Southport FC. Since the Millennium, however, the leagues have contracted as teams are dropping out. Young people are just not joining things anymore, something drama groups, social clubs and other organisations are only too well aware of.

I have taken up after dinner speaking too.

But about the writing…

I've written seven Johnny Ace crime novels set around Southport and Merseyside about a Liverpool DJ/Private Eye and. Plus two more DCI Glass mysteries and two volumes of poetry, one of which won the national 1992 Sefton Poetry Competition.

I've also branched out into publishing. In 2004 I brought out Spencer Leigh's history of Merseybeat & The Beatles, entitled 'Twist & Shout', under my Nirvana Books imprint and other authors have followed.

And, with local house prices rising faster than London ones, I have started buying property, small terraced houses, in Southport again.

So, at the age of 65, Ron is down to six jobs, which to him seems like retirement.

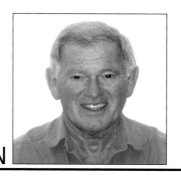

RONNIE FEARN

Possibly Southport's best-known resident, Lord Ronnie Fearn was born at 99 Clifton Road on February 2nd 1931 and was educated at Norwood Road School and King George V Grammar School. He joined Southport Borough Council in 1963 and has served continuously on the council ever since. From 1987-92 he was Liberal M.P. for Southport and returned as Liberal Democrat MP from 1997-2001.

Ronnie has also had parallel careers in banking and as a voluntary youth leader. He has been a leading light of All Souls Drama Group since its inception in 1949 and has appeared in and directed many of their productions.

Like practically everyone in Southport, I have known Ronnie Fearn for years. We once did the soft shoe shuffle together on the stage of the Floral Hall on a Sixties Reunion Night and, on another occasion, he tried to sell me the Gladstone Liberal Club in Sussex Road.

Considering his incredible work schedule, even at the age of 74, I was lucky to get a morning with him at his Norwood Avenue home the week before Easter 2005. He had just returned from a select committee trip to Poland and Germany.

We started off talking about his acting career.

I attended KGV School from 1942-49. I was in the First XI at Rugby and I was keen on athletics but my real passion was the Drama Society. One of the plays I appeared in was 'Richard of Bordeaux'. Mr. Millward, the then headmaster, was involved and, later, our English master, George Wakefield directed and produced the plays.

I went to Sunday School at All Souls in Norwood Road and became leader of the Youth Club at 15, a post I held for 21 years. I had my first pint of beer at the Belle Vue Hotel on Lord Street West, which was where all the posh teenagers went at the time and which featured small bands. But most of my time was spent at All Souls which was one of the three top youth clubs in the town, the others being St. Cuthbert's, run by John Cotterall and Denis Braddock, and Our Lady of Lourdes run by Joe Sweeney.

After the War, we formed the All Souls Dramatic Club and put shows on in the hall. We also went on tour playing in church halls and farm buildings around the area as far away as Hoscar. We made curtains out of blackout material. I was a writer, producer and actor.

The official All Souls Dramatic Club was formed in the early 1950's and went from strength to strength. From doing a show over three nights, we went to a week's run then on to two weeks. Every night we had to put the chairs away after the performance only to have to put them out again the next day. We performed one-acts and an annual pantomime in which I usually played the Dame. Eventually, in the 1970's, we moved over to the Arts Centre where we still hold the pantomimes in January every year, playing to over 4000 people.

I well remember the first show when the roof of the stage blew off in a gale during the performance.

I wrote a one-act play called 'Wind in my Sails' as All Souls entry in the Southport Drama Festival and once appeared at the Scala Theatre in 'The Trial of Mary Dugan' along with Jean Alexander.

Ronnie did his two years National Service in the Navy, serving on HMS Illustrious in the Korea crisis. When he returned he went back to All Souls.

When I was a teenager in the late forties and early fifties, local music venues like the Floral Hall, the Casino (Old Tyme), the Scala and the Palace Hotel, all featured bands playing strict tempo dance music. We used to go to Fozzards in Tulketh Street where they served hot soft drinks and Uncle Macs in Seabank Road after night school.

When skiffle and rock'n'roll came into vogue in the late Fifties, we ran dances at All Souls on a Saturday night featuring beat groups like The Teenbeats, The Rebel Rousers and Sandy Shore & The Beach Boys. There were lots of social events in the town at that time, like the annual Transport Ball at the Palace Hotel, and there were 36 youth clubs in Southport compared with just four today.

Ronnie joined the Young Liberals in the early sixties and soon put up for Southport Town Council, winning Craven Ward seat from the Conservatives in 1963 and becoming one of just three Liberals elected.

I was on the Fire & Ambulance and Parks and Cemeteries committees. The ethos of the day was 'don't raise the rates or you'll lose the votes' and, as a result, the infrastructure of the town was suffering. We were the first party to offer free travel passes. I now serve as a cabinet member for Leisure and Tourism.

Throughout all this, of course, I was working for the Royal Bank of Scotland, previously William Deacons and Williams & Glyns Bank. My career as a bank official took me to Ormskirk, Ainsdale and Southport where I became Chairman of the local Institute of Bankers. I was also raised to Fellow of the Institute of Bankers in later years.

Ronnie became the Liberal Democrat Leader of Sefton Borough Council and Merseyside County Council before standing for Parliament in 1987 when he won the Southport seat from the Conservative incumbent, Sir Ian Percival, with 48% of the vote. He served for five years before being ousted by a new Conservative candidate, Matthew Banks, in 1992. However, Ronnie regained the seat from Mr Banks at the 1997 election. When he stood down in 2001, Dr John Pugh held Southport for the Lib-Dems and was successful again in the 2005 election against the new Tory candidate, Mark Bigley.

Meanwhile, in 1985, Ronnie was awarded an OBE for services to the community

My maiden speech in Parliament was, of course, on Tourism. I spent ten years at the House of Commons where I used to receive 600 letters a week. In Parliament, on a private member's bill, I successfully campaigned for rear seat belts for children in cars. I was party spokesman for Housing, Health, Transport and Tourism.

Ronnie was made a life peer in 2001. Now Lord Fearn, he is still actively involved in public life and after 41 years in local government and 10 years as an M.P., I asked him what he regarded as his greatest local achievements.

I helped to save the G.P.O. in Lord Street and worked for the restoration of the Pier. I also fought for the refurbishment of Hesketh Park through the Victorian Parks Heritage, English Heritage and the Lottery and, at the same time, helped save Southport's baby unit at the Christiana Hartley Maternity Hospital.

I regret I was not able to save the original bandstand in the Municipal Gardens.

Ronnie is married to Joyce. They have two children and five grandchildren and still live at Blowick. At the age of 75, Ronnie is as energetic as ever and shows no signs of retiring. He is obviously a man who enjoys life and who thinks Southport is the greatest place on earth. I wouldn't disagree with that.

HARRY FOSTER

Harry Foster is the fifth generation of his family born in Southport, in Harry's case in June 1931 at 167 Upper Aughton Road. Alongside a career as a lecturer in education, he has written nine books on the history of the town.

I had never met Harry Foster although I own three of his excellent books on Southport's history. When he invited me to his home, I found it to be a treasure-trove of Southport memorabilia as, indeed, were his own memories.

My grandfather was a thatcher and my father was a Sand Inspector for Southport Corporation. His job was to ticket builders who collected sand from the beach and weigh it in at the weighbridge by the Cheshire Lines station at the Birkdale Palace Hotel. He would have his mid-day break with the Marshside fishermen who worked the water chute at Pleasureland.

Later, my parents had an off licence on the corner of Mosley Street and Banastre Road. From the age of three, I went to Bury Road council school where Miss Mitchell was the head mistress. It was the first school in Southport to have a purpose-built nursery. I then transferred to Linaker Street at nine and on to KGV in 1942 under Mr. Millward.

The rugby teams were decided on weight and height. I was so big I went straight into playing with the seniors. The games master, Harry Smith, who was at Waterloo Rugby Club, introduced boxing at the school in 1946 and he took me to play at Waterloo.

Harry went on to play rugby for Lancashire in the County Championship winning side and was an England XV reserve.

When I was a student, I had summer jobs like everyone else. I worked on the Pier. When Tommy Cooper was appearing in town, he used to walk down the Pier every day and always gave the attendants a toffee. We helped the electricians who were putting lights up on the decorative loops. The corporation were trying to cut costs. Instead of buying coloured bulbs, they bought the cheaper plain ones and we had to paint them different colours. We hadn't got the weatherproof sealant and when Sir Herbert Barber switched on the lights on round about 1950, it started to rain and all the lights fused and went out.

We did overtime working in the Municipal Gardens where there was open-air dancing to Jimmy Leach and his Organolians.

Harry studied at Sheffield University and Chester College before going on to teach at Farnborough Road School in 1952.

I taught juniors for eight years. Colin Alty, who played football for Southport, was one of my pupils as was Jimmy Rimmer, the Manchester United and England goalkeeper. I moved to Freshfield County Primary School as deputy head in 1960.

About 1965, there was a rapid expansion in teacher training. Edgar Johns (Churchtown headmaster) and myself were nominated by the local authority as potential lecturers and I was offered a post at Edge Hill teacher training college in Ormskirk.

Harry was also involved in youth work in the evenings at Meols Cop Youth Centre.

This was one of the civic centres run by the local authority. Bob Abram was at Birkdale Secondary School, John Cottterall ran Stanley and I was a Warden at Meols Cop from 1960 to 1965. We opened three nights a week and had about 100 teenagers coming down. We used the school facilities at the time I was there but a purpose built centre was erected in the 1970's. Eric Gale, who taught at KGV, ran a basketball team and Teddy 'Snowball' Aspinall was in charge of boxing though dancing to pop records was the favoured activity. Teddy was a groundsman for Southport Education Authority but he also ran a boxing academy in the old stables behind the Bold Hotel on Lord Street.

Harry spent the rest of his working life at Edge Hill College, becoming a Head of Department. Whilst there he gained an M.A. and PhD from Liverpool University for local research. He retired from lecturing in 1989 but all the time he had a secondary 'career' as a local historian.

It started off helping my students who had to teach local history in Southport schools. I put postcards and other pictures on to slides that I also used when I gave talks to church and other groups. I gave about six talks every winter for forty years. In the late 1970's, Sylvia Harrap founded the Southport & Birkdale Historical Research Society and wrote the book on Old Birkdale and Ainsdale, which was based on the University Extension course she ran. I joined the society and brought the history up to date with my book on New Birkdale, taking it from 1850 where Sylvia's history had stopped. Histories of Ainsdale, Crossens, the fishing industry and the Flower Show followed.

Harry was involved in various other activities round the town.

I was a trustee at the Kent Road Methodist Church, which closed in the early 1970's. It used to be a thriving church with a Sunday School and a scout troop. We regularly enjoyed going to weekend camp at Tawd Vale.

In 1995, I became captain of Hesketh Golf Club and wrote a history of the club which is the oldest in the town. Originally known as Southport Golf Club, the course was built in 1885 adjacent to the notorious Little Ireland settlement. Indeed, the green keeper's cottage used to be the old Protestant School. In 1892, the club moved to a newly constructed course at Moss Lane in 1892 but returned to the now fallow land after the Little Ireland settlement was demolished in 1885. The Moss Lane course became the Old Links. Golf courses attract developers and the new young landowner, Bibby Hesketh, offered 20% discount on club fees to people who bought leases on his newly built properties in Hesketh Road. All the houses had gates leading to the gold course at the end of their gardens and quite often stray balls landed in the gardens. One pair of adjoining houses had contrasting notices by their gates, 'Golfers Keep Out' and 'Golfers Welcome'.

Harry has also been president of Southport Rotary Club, which meets every Wednesday lunchtime at the Royal Clifton Hotel. At 75, he still plays golf and is currently writing histories of Southport & Ainsdale and Royal Birkdale Golf Clubs. He and his wife live close to Hesketh Golf Club.

RALPH GREGSON

Ralph Gregson was born in Widnes on January 1st 1931 but came to Southport when he was 16. He is best known as the founder of the Birkdale Civic Society.

I had met Ralph on odd occasions over the years but his name was rarely out of the papers for his efforts to promote tourism in Southport. In his elegant Birkdale lounge, he reminisced about his career and the people he had met.

I was meant to be a solicitor but after one month as a clerk at Loveridge & Moore's in Hoghton Street in 1947, I left to join Southport Corporation in the Publicity & Attractions Dept. I stayed until 1952 with a break for National Service in the RAF in between.

In 1952, Ralph sought to further his career in the tourism industry by taking a post as Entertainments Manager at Hayes in Middlesex but he returned to Southport Corporation in 1954 when he was put in charge of the Cambridge Hall, the Pier and the Municipal Gardens for a salary of £500 per annum. Alderman Thornley was the chairman of the P. & A. committee at the time and George Rimmer had succeeded Leslie Bedford as head of the department.

There was a lot going on in the Municipal Gardens in those days. Jimmy Leech and his Organolians were the resident band and we could get up to a thousand people dancing until midnight. We had Morris Dancing and an outdoor quiz game based on TV's 'Take Your Pick'.

Out of season, events were held inside the Cambridge Hall, which could hold up to 900 people. We had the Belle of the Ball beauty contest that pre-dated the English Rose and in which the contestants wore gowns rather than bathing suits. There was Old Tyme dancing and, of course, it was used as a venue for smaller conferences or an overspill from the Floral Hall. We had movable loom seats for shows but there was permanent seating on the balcony.

Despite his interest in tourism, Ralph allowed a friend to persuade him to apply with him for a job in the buying department of Littlewoods stores.

Unfortunately for him, it was me who got offered the job and I accepted because it paid £100 a year more than I was getting at the Publicity & Attractions.

Ralph stayed with Littlewoods for 27 years during which time he travelled all over the world sourcing material for the knitwear department.

Basically, I was in the rag trade. I must have been to Hong Kong over thirty times in all. It was a great life and they were a good company to work for. When I told them I wanted to go into local politics, they gave me their blessing as they were keen on people putting something back into the community but it was noticeable that I didn't start getting promotions until I gave up my seat.

How it started was this. Ronnie Fearn and Bob Hughes came to see me in the late 1960's and asked me if I'd stand for the council as the Liberal candidate for Southport West. I wasn't really into politics and declined but in 1971 I was approached again, this time by Keith Mitchell for the Conservatives, and I agreed to join their ward committee. In 1971, I won the same seat, beating the Liberal candidate who was Bessie Eaton of June's Florists.

I was twelve years on the council, representing Birkdale & Ainsdale after the 1974 shake-up. During that time, I was chairman of the Tourism & Attractions Dept as it was now called; ironic when you think I left thee as a mere assistant. In 1986 I knew my number was up. That was the year of the 20% rate increase and the Tories were decimated countrywide. Sefton Council has been a hung council ever since and that is one of its problems. I voted to belong to Lancashire and, despite massive lobbying by Sefton, we only lost the decision by three votes.

Ralph turned his attention from public life to the voluntary sector. He was the founder chairman of Oxfam in Southport.

With the help of Michael Wolfe, vicar of St Paul's, and his wife Brenda, we rented an empty shop in Chapel Street in 1964. Actress Patricia Wymark performed the opening ceremony. We were the first charity shop in Southport and our main objective was fundraising. We held chairs in the Municipal Gardens and coffee mornings and we moved premises from one empty shop after another as leases became taken up. Eventually, in 1976, we moved to 93 Eastbank Street to where the Alamir Restaurant is today. We took £300 in our first week and the rent was only £1.50p.

In 1986, we relocated in bigger premises at 26 London Street where we are today but we have competition for 19 other charity shops whilst stores like Tesco and Matalan with their cheap prices mean we have had to accept less for many of our goods.

By now, Oxfam have become shop operators with a huge property division and Ralph just acts as a voluntary consultant on retailing but he has plenty else to occupy his time.

I was Chairman of governors at Farnborough Road Infants, which is the largest in the country with 500 children aged between 5 and 7 years old. There were another 500 in the junior school.

Ralph had been in the Boys Brigade at St. Paul's Church since he was a boy and now he is Vice-President of the Southport Battalion.

The Boys Brigade is a Christian organisation, always attached to a particular church although not Roman Catholic ones. It offers moral training and discipline and teaches drill, citizenship, scripture, first aid, arts and crafts and sports. Boys join from 12 to 18. We used to have 30-40 boys in the company but nowadays, like many institutions, numbers have fallen drastically. We now have only a dozen members and they tend to leave earlier, at 16.

Ralph's biggest interest of all is the Birkdale Civic Society, which he founded in 1983 and it all came about by accident.

Twelve trees in Birkdale Village, many of them 60-70 years old, had died of Dutch Elm disease. Sefton Council said they could not afford to replace them but if I could stump up £250 (£20 a tree), they would agree to do the work. I took it upon myself to write to all the shopkeepers and residents in the area asking for donations and we collected an amazing £850, which we used to buy benches, litter bins and street furniture as well as the trees,

I realised the strength of feeling in Birkdale about the Village and invited interested parties to a meeting at the Birkdale Conservative Club. Thirty people turned up and the Civic Society was born. Our big achievement was to persuade the council to make the village a conservation area.

The society has access to Birkdale planning applications and sets up partnership schemes with Sefton Council.

In the 1990's, we took a landlocked derelict site that ran between Pleasureland and Weld Road behind Victoria Park and created the Queens Jubilee Nature Trail. People used to ride motorbikes and horses over it and it was full of rubbish. 200 people turned up to help clear it and McDonalds provided free drinks. We raised £20,000 from various quangos, Hamilton Oil gave a donation, and we ended up receiving a Higher Citation, which the Queen presented to me in November 1992.

Our current project is the construction of Southport Eco Centre on beside that same land. It will be an energy garden with interactive exhibitions for children.

Birkdale Civic Society now has sixty members who meet every six weeks at Ralph Gregson's home. But, if you want to join, be warned. There is a waiting list.

MIKE HALSALL

Mike Halsall, founder of Halsall Heating Services Ltd., was born in Southport on 9th February 1943. He is a Member of the Southport Rotary Club, the President of the Southport YMCA and was a Conservative Town Councillor in the time of the Southport County Borough Council.

When Mike started his central heating business I was one of his first customers when he installed an oil-fired heating system in my house in Moss Lane, Churchtown, but I also knew him from our schooldays together at KGV Grammar School.

I started my schooldays at the Churchtown Nursery School, which was, at the time was housed in the old Congregational Hall off Botanic Road, I moved on to Churchtown Junior School and then to KGV to complete my education. In the holidays, at weekends and after school I worked as a Lifeguard on the Southport Beach, working with the amphibious DUKW'S, I also did a Saturday butchers round for Mr Taylor at Billington's Butchers in Manchester Road as well as paper rounds for Blacklins, Thornbers and the local Post Office.

After leaving school I trained as a design draughtsman with Mather and Platt in Manchester (1960-63) then worked for North West Gas (1963-69) as a Sales Student eventually becoming a central heating designer based in Liverpool and later Southport. I then left the Gas Board to join a Liverpool heating company, Ashley and McDonough of Huyton, as their Sales Manager. During this time I studied Business and Marketing at the Liverpool College of Commerce in Tithebarn Street attaining Membership of the Chartered Institute of Marketing.

Mike owed his start in business indirectly to Peter McCabe who ran a successful electrical business in Birkdale Village.

I was a member of Southport Round Table No 43 and I was responsible for organising a charity fund raising event called "Jazz on the Moss" at Olversons Farm at Scarisbrick. I asked Peter, as an ex-Tabler, to assist in setting up the electrics for the event. Unknown to me Peter had a problem; central heating was just coming into vogue and McCabe's were not equipped to handle it effectively so he asked me if I could help him by designing his heating systems.

In practice Peter lent me one of his fitters, David Rothwell, who later married my cousin, Carole, and with McCabe's support Halsall Heating was born.

I started Halsall Heating from my home in Grange Road in December 1971 and ran it from there for the first few months before moving to the old Co-op shop at 28 Hesketh Drive Southport. One of our first jobs was to install central heating for a friend, Andrew Greenhalgh at his home in Rutland Road. When the job was finished Andrew pushed a cheque through my front door, which was promptly eaten by our dog, a great start!

In 1971 most houses wanted gas fires or gas boilers although many had coal fires with back boilers heating radiators and hot water. Paraffin stoves had all but died out. About 60% of our heating systems were gas fired with the rest using oil, solid fuel or electricity.

In those days a central heating system for a 3-bed semi cost about £400 roughly the cost of a new Mini Car, Today, the cost of the same system would cost around £4000 but a new "mini" costs £10000. A tribute to the efficiency of our industry.

Whilst talking about efficiency, in 1971 we were proud of our gas boilers being able to attain a combustion efficiency of 55-60%, in 2006 we expect our gas boilers to be over 90% efficient, a huge saving in fuel bills. In the70's our main competition was from Norman Ibbotson's Select Heating, J A Brooks and Chas Hill, whose slogan was "By Hill its Hot" Our first big contract was for Derek Howard, installing the heating and plumbing in Hollyhurst Lodge, a large block of flats in Weld Road, Birkdale.

We have also been involved in designing and installing many heating systems for churches, which have always been notoriously cold buildings. They were traditionally heated all of the winter with a coke boiler, which would be stoked twice a day to heat pipework in underfloor ducts with heat rising through floor grills. Later many of these boilers were converted to oil firing with time clocks so that the systems could be switched on and off automatically. Nowadays, gas-fired boilers are installed serving fan convectors, which can provide a rapid heat up with an even distribution of warmth throughout the building. By heating the perimeter of the church the centre of the church is kept warm, the same principle as having radiators under the windows in your home.

In 1979 we moved premises to Shakespeare Street, by which time we had 25 staff, today we have over 40.

Away from work, Mike works in a voluntary capacity for the YMCA, he is the President of the Southport YMCA, the Chairman of the North West Region and he has national responsibilities.

Originally, the YMCA took over the old Girls Club to support girls in service. I first joined the YMCA when I was 14 in order to take lessons in ballroom dancing. There were just three of us in the class that was held in a large room at the top of a stone staircase in the old YMCA premises at the corner of Queen Anne Street and Eastbank Street. In those days the YMCA was more of a social club providing leisure activities such as table tennis and dances similar to the youth clubs of the time. Although the YM still provides the traditional activities it now concerns itself more with health and fitness, gymnastics and, most important of all, social welfare, working with young people in times of need, helping with housing, unemployment and drug problems and providing nursery facilities. The club needs to make a profit as the only funding comes from local government agencies.

When we moved to the new Hoghton Street building, I'd become involved on the management side. Before becoming YM President, I was Chairman of the North West region.

As well as his involvement with the YMCA Movement, Mike has also been Chairman and President of Southport Round Table, a School Governor for many years, whilst for a time in the seventies; he pursued a career in local politics.

I was asked by Councillor Ralph Earp to stand for Talbot Ward (now part of Norwood Ward) and I won the seat in 1970 taking over from Councillor Jean Leech who was elevated to the Aldermanic Bench. I served on the Education Committee and as Deputy Chairman of Town Planning in which capacity I was involved in the Conservation Order for Lord Street. In 1974 I was not able to stand again as due to Local Government Reorganisation, with the formation of Sefton I would have had to serve on two Councils in the same year which was an impossibility for me with a young family and a growing business.

In 2005, Mike sold his business to CPL Heating and Plumbing of Preston, a company that Mike believes will look after his loyal customers and staff, and he is now enjoying his retirement in his Churchtown home.

DAVID HARRISON

David Harrison was born in Ainsdale in 1936 and was the manager of the Moulin Rouge ballroom in the 1960's and 70's..

The Moulin Rouge was one of my favourite venues as a DJ in the Seventies. Apart from playing there regularly, I used to call in on my way back from a gig in Liverpool for a bacon sandwich and a cup of tea, the only place you could get such a thing at one o'clock n the morning.

I always found David Harrison to be a charming and urbane man, usually surrounded by voluptuous girls and always recognizable by his shades. When I met him again at his Ainsdale home over thirty years later, I found he had not changed.

I've always been an Ainsdale boy. I went to school at Ainsdale St. Johns, then Birkdale Central and finally the Technical College in Southport where I studied Brickwork and Steel. Little Mr. Walwyn was the headmaster and he ruled with a rod of iron.

In 1952, I became an apprentice at Raytax Photographic Services in South Road Waterloo for a wage of £4 a week. The return fare from Ainsdale on the Ribble bus was nine pence halfpenny.

As a young lad, I did odd jobs at the Plaza Cinema. They paid me half a crown for going in at 10.15 on a Sunday night after the last show and rewinding the film to send back to the publishers so they could swap the cans over and I reloaded the next week's film.

Above the cinema there was a little dance hall and café selling tea and biscuits. Seats cost 6d in the first 8 rows, 1/6d in the middle and 2/3d in the 'snogging rows'. Groups came to the dance hall. Clarkson Woods played there and the Panama Jazz Band.

The Plaza struggled because they couldn't get the latest films and, by the sixties, television was killing off cinemas everywhere. Only the big chains survived.

Ainsdale was a very sociable place in the early fifties. Quite a number of local church members from St. John's would meet up at Ye Olde Tea Shoppe for tea and hot chocolate after Sunday School. From here, many outings were organized. A coach to Blackpool, a favourite destination, cost five shillings.

Friday nights would see the same crowd at either the Congregational Church Hall for play rehearsals and dancing to records or the Plaza Cinema Ballroom for a tea dance. At weekends they had a small dance band.

In the daytimes, we were often found at the Ainsdale Cricket and Tennis Club. The Ainsdale Flower Show in those days was held on the recreation ground on Liverpool Road opposite Oakwood Avenue.

There were boats on the lake behind the Lakeside Hotel (now The Sands). They used to charge 5d to hire a canoe, 8d for a rowing boat and 1/6d for a motor boat. When I was 14, I used to help pull the boats into the shed at the back of the hotel at night.

In 1954, David was called up for National Service and when he came out he joined Southport Police.

Harold Mighall was the Chief Constable and O'Keefe was Chief Super-intendent. I covered the whole county borough from Crossens to Woodvale Bridge during my two-year probation. I did a stint at Ainsdale station then went mobile on the motorbikes. We rode Triumph 500's and the plugs would get furred up with driving round town so we zipped up and down the Formby by-pass to blow away the cobwebs..

I suggested to David that policing the town in those days was different to how it is done today.

We'd spend the night walking round our beats trying every shop, factory and office door and it was a sin not to find one unlocked. If a car was stolen, Belisha beacons flashed. You'd find a stolen car on your beat about once every six months on average. The villains preferred a clip round the ear rather than going to court. Couldn't do it now. You'd get arrested yourself. But the streets were safer then. Now it's horrendous.

Benny Hartwell was the Magistrates Clerk. He'd ask the defendant, 'How did you get to court this morning?' 'On my bike,' they'd say. 'Well you better go out and sell your bike to pay your fine.' If they asked for time to pay, he'd nod amiably and say, 'Certainly. 24 hours.'.

J. Paynes of Llandudno bought the old Plaza Cinema in 1956. Charlie Payne was friendly with the Chief Constable. Charlie was Mayor of Llandudno, Chairman of the Magistrates and owned three hotels in Llandudno and the Palace in Rhyl. He refurbished the Plaza, converted it into a ballroom and opened up in 1957 as The Moulin Rouge.

Jim Pendlebury was manager of the Moulin Rouge. Jim had a pilot's licence and he used to take me flying at Woodvale. He'd join us in the Police Crown

Green Bowling Competitions. My wife, Judith, was working at the Moulin Rouge. I wasn't allowed to have another job, being in the police, but I helped out on promotions. One day, Judith came home at 2am one morning and woke me up to tell me Jim Pendlebury was leaving. 'It'd be the perfect job for you,' she said. I agreed and resigned from the police. It was 1967.

When I applied for the first 2am licence in Southport, the Benny Hartwell said, 'We know Mr. Harrison.I don't think we need to ask any questions.' And the licence was granted. John James at the Kingsway got his licence the same day, 1am weekdays and 2am Friday and Saturday. I got a 2am upstairs in the Latin Room, 11pm in the ballroom downstairs and 10.30pm in the Windmill bar, which had been a private club. Stuart Fish from Brighouses was my solicitor. He later became a recorder in Manchester and he soon got me a 2am licence throughout the building.

There was a large communal entrance to the Moulin Rouge leading to a beautiful carpeted foyer with wooden panels on the walls. On either side of the entrance were two shops.

On the extreme left was a barber's shop run by a cricketer from Ainsdale Club called Norman Toft who used a runner as he had short legs.

On the other side was a sweet and tobacconists and next door to that was an umbrella maker and repairer who opened two days a week.

They all paid rent to the Moulin Rouge Company.

The ballroom could accommodate 800 people. It had a sprung floor purchased by Charlie Payne from an old ballroom in Bolton. The stage was where the old cinema screen had been.

When we had a big function, we erected a marquee in the car park until finally, we built an extension. People came to the Moulin from all over the County.

Ronnie Bateman was the resident band in the ballroom with dancing from 8pm to 11.30pm .when people would move upstairs to the disco. Stan Moreton used to play the organ. Admission was 4/6 (3/6d on production of the Visiter advert), climbing up to ten shillings after decimalisation.

The jukebox in the Latin Lounge was the first stereo juke box in the country and it earned a fortune for us.

I was chairman and secretary of the Licensed Victuallers Association and I used to book some of my acts through Billy 'Uke' Scott's agency and he sent Tom O'Connor to perform at a Licensed Victuallers' event for a special fee of £15. Tom had ridden on the Pier Train earlier in the evening in a silver grey silk suit in pouring rain and the suit shrunk before he came to us.

The Arts Ball was held at the Moulin for seven years. They spent the whole of Friday decking the place out using a different theme each year, once an autumn scene with leaves everywhere and another time a quarry. One year, Fleetwood Mac was their star act.

George Melly was a regular as were The Merseysippi and the Panama Jazz Bands. We had Syd Lawrence and his Orchestra for £410, Ross Jackson supplied all the sound equipment for us. He had a shop in Bispham Road and was a brilliant sound man. He invented something called tunnel sound that put maximum sound through a speaker before it blew up.

The Moulin Rouge closed in 1976, The Payne's empire ran into financial difficulty and sold out to Mecca for £27,000 who gutted the building and reopened it as Tiffany's. They sent David on a training course and kept him on as manager. Judith, who'd been in a secretarial post at the Moulin, took over the bookings.

They'd ruined the place. That beautiful interior became very plastic. They stopped the ballroom dancing and brought in Mecca registered bands and DJ's and introduced Miss World contests. Hal Robbins ran the resident band. Soon there were drugs, fights and under-age drinking and I got out.

David left to work at Park Hall, Chorley but soon returned to Southport to run The Snooty Fox bar in the Royal Clifton Hotel, which was owned by the Prince of Wales Group at the time. John Trisconnia was general manager.

Ken Dodd performed the opening ceremony with me. There was a full sized snooker table and, at lunchtimes, Little Billy played the piano. At night they had groups and discos and it was very popular but it became a gathering for people leaving Pleasureland and became very rough. I was glad to be head hunted by Phil Melville to run the bar at Southport Squash Club.

The boiler there was the biggest coal boiler in the UK and, as well as the Baths, it used to heat the water for Caves the Chemist in Neville Street.

Unfortunately, there were too many people running the show.

Tiffany's, meanwhile, had been bought out by two Liverpool men who opened it up as Ainsdale Country Club but the problems that had troubled Tiffanys continued and, before long, the building was knocked down altogether and was replaced by the Natterjack pub which stands there today.

David spent a short time at Southport Squash Club, which has been opened in the old Victoria Baths by a group of Southport businessmen led by Tony Rodwell.

In the early 1980's, he joined Ian Wyman's Integroup Communications company in Hoghton Street selling telecommunication and sound systems. He was there for fifteen years and became a director. Now part retired, he chauffeurs celebrities and business executives.

GORDON HEROD

Gordon Herod is a jazz musician, actor and former detective. For many years, he ran the miniature train and the boats in Botanic Gardens. He was born in Dukinfield on May 19th 1933 and came to Southport in 1953 when he joined the Southport County Borough Police. I visited him in February 2006 at his Marshside home where he lives with his wife, Enid.

I first knew Gordon by his stage name, Eric Sampson. We used to meet up at Granada TV when we were both extras on programmes like 'Coronation Street' and 'Sherlock Holmes'.

I'd been a police cadet and in the Military Police since I was 16. When I came to Southport as a constable, we used to direct the traffic at The Monument and at the Lord Street-Eastbank Street junction. Police cars were Humber Hawks fitted with two-way radios with an operator at HQ back at the station.

I was Court Officer from 1956-61 then went into CID as a Fingerprint and Photo Officer. In 1969, Southport combined with Lancashire County and I was made up to Detective Sergeant. That was an excellent force but they made the big mistake of leaving Lancashire in 1974 and going in with Merseyside.

I worked on the Charlie Griffiths murder. Charlie was an old man who was trussed up and beaten to death in his shop in Eastbank Street. The case was never solved. And I was involved on a case in Manchester Road when a baby was beaten to death. One suspect pinched my gloves out of my pocket in the Rabbit Inn in Manchester Road. I found them in his house and nicked him but when I put the theft charge up to my superiors they said 'you must be joking'. But I got my gloves back.

We went on early morning arrests for people who hadn't paid their fines. One man came to the door wearing only a vest that barely covered his naval. He asked if he could go upstairs and put some clothes on. We said yes but when he came back, all he'd put on was a pair of socks.

Gordon formed the Police Dance Band in 1959 to play at police functions but he soon started getting bookings from outside the force.

So when we did those gigs, we went out as the Eric Sampson Band but we were all policemen. The line-up was guitar, piano, clarinet/sax and drums, with myself on trumpet. The band kept going until 1975 and we played all the local venues like the Midnight Lounge at the Floral Hall and the Marine View at the Queens Hotel.

In 1975, I met up with Denny Kirkpatrick and we formed the Denny Gordon Duo, working for the Tony West Agency in Crosby. That lasted 12 years. At the same time, we also went out as a 6-piece trad jazz band and did a 3-year residency at the Marine Club.

For 12 years, I was compére of the Tetley Search for a Star auditions at the Floral Hall and I introduced the National Youth Jazz Orchestra for their first concerts at the Floral Hall and Arts Centre for the charity Bacchus who held their meetings at the old Richmond Hotel in Scarisbrick New Road. I was vice-chairman of the North West area.

Gordon left the police service in 1978 and had the idea of resurrecting boating on the lake at the Botanic Gardens. He approached Sefton Council who granted him a licence to run the operation.

The Southport Naval Cadets gave me a hand cleaning the lake. Using mesh nets, we pulled out over five tons of rubbish. I rebuilt the boathouse and the boat store. I bought some boats from Tommy Mann, who was running the Marine Lake, and others from Ferranti's in North Wales. They were fibreglass rowing boats. I also acquired the old Southport lifeboat, which was kept at the end of the Pier, and converted it into a 12-seater pleasure boat with the passengers seated round the sides. We opened in Easter 1979 with a dozen boats. Later I introduced canoes and safety paddleboats for children.

Not content with being in charge of water transport at the Botanic, Gordon soon turned his attention to the travel possibilities on land.

I'd noticed a lot of old people couldn't get around the gardens so easily on foot so I had the idea of running one of those 'petite-trains' that you see on the Continent. The Council liked the idea so I bought an engine that ran on electric batteries and, with my brother's help, built a couple of coaches, one open and one with a canopy. We opened in May 1983 and charged 40p for adults and 20p for children for a round tour of the gardens. It's still going strong today.

Six years later, Gordon's travel empire expanded to Hesketh Park where he set up a similar operation.

We painted the train with a blue and yellow livery and set up a ticket office inside the old pagoda that had fallen into disrepair. We just opened on weekends and holidays in Hesketh Park but in 1991, something went amiss with the valve at the end of the lake and nearly all the water drained out by mistake. We lost many of the fish and so much water that you couldn't sail the boats on it anymore. It was a sea of mud. I packed it in then.

Gordon kept the Botanic Gardens operation going until 2000 when he retired after 21 years there.

I still carried on with the TV work for a couple of years and got a few walk-on parts. My best job was playing a police commander in a film starring Rod Steiger and Anthony Perkins, both of whom are now dead. Now I've given that up too.

I thought it was a pity Gordon was insistent about retiring as I could see an opening for him to bring his 'petite train' out of mothballs and run a much needed service from the town centre to Ocean Plaza for those many people whose legs were unable to make the long, windswept trek to the town's only cinema.

TREVOR HITCHEN

Trevor Hitchen was born in Sowerby Bridge, Yorkshire in 1926. He joined Southport FC on New Years Eve 1948 and played for them for seven and a half seasons. He returned in 1958 to manage the club for six months and then moved to Formby FC where he started off as player-manager and ended up as Chairman, a post he held for four years.

He opened his first newsagents business in 1950 in Coronation Walk. In 1955, he took over the kiosk at the Ribble Bus Station which he ran for 12 years whence he bought Smithies newsagents in Hoghton Street where he stayed until his retirement in 1987.

I preceded Trevor at Haig Avenue by 18 months. I attended my first football match at the age of five in August 1947, the first game of a new season. Southport, playing in green and white hoops, were beaten 4-0 by Stockport County, an ominous omen for the future. By the time Trevor joined, in the following season, I was a regular supporter.

Over tea and biscuits at his Birkdale home in 2005, Trevor told me how he started at the old Third Division North club.

Mr. Rayner was the chairman when I joined Southport FC. He owned fishmongers in Eastbank Street and one next to Birkdale Station. Gordon Hunt was the secretary. I lodged with Mrs Brunt in Haig Avenue when I first came to the town then moved to digs in Cross Street with a Mrs May Ball.

I played for the club for seven and a half seasons; usually at inside forward or wing half although for the last fifteen matches they played me at left back.

Trevor was the most amenable footballer who ever played for Southport. He would play in whatever position they asked him and never quibbled. Even when he was sacked as manager, on the very day that he brought in £400 to hand over to the Development Committee, he shook hands with the board and agreed to stay on to help the new incumbent.

Over five thousand turned up to see Stanley Matthews, Nat Lofthouse and other stars play in Trevor's testimonial in 1954 to commemorate his five years of loyal service to the club.

When Gordon Hunt dropped my wages by £2 a week I went to Oldham Athletic. It was 1955 and I bought my first car, a Hillman Minx, for the travelling. It cost £500. After 12 months, Sam Barkas signed me for Wigan Athletic who were in the Lancashire Combination. When Sam was sacked, I took over as player manager and we came to Southport in the FA Cup and beat them in front of a 14,000 crowd.

In 1958, Mr Fernley of Rotten Row asked me to take over as manager at Southport. It wasn't a good time. Two star players, George Bromilow and Wally Taylor, had just left and there was no money in the kitty to replace them, I had a £200 a week total wage bill and I was running four teams. I knew that the only way forward was to go for youth. But after six months they brought Wally Fielding. I stayed on a bit longer to help him find his feet but then moved to Formby F.C.

I'd coached at Formby whilst I was at Southport. Their President was Mr Glass who owned Holmwood School in Freshfield. He asked me to go there as player manager. Formby were in the Liverpool County League. I stayed until 1966 when I hung up my boots. I was 40 years old. Later, I became chairman of the club when Gerry Walker resigned and I stayed for four years. Brian Griffiths was the manager.

I carried on coaching Ainsdale youth teams, though, right up to 1996.

My own first dealings with Trevor were in my days as a DJ when he was chairman of Formby FC in their old Brows Lane ground. He used to book me to run the weekly discos in the clubhouse. But I was also a regular customer at his shops, in the Ribble Bus Station and, later, at Smithies.

Concurrent with his career as a footballer, Trevor had been building up his newsagents' business and he was to become a very well known retailer in the town.

I ran my own paper round when I was a lad in Halifax so when a teammate at Southport, Jack Rothwell, asked me to go in with him in a newsagents shop, previously owned by a Mr. Firth. I didn't hesitate..

We opened up in Coronation Walk in 1950, next to Madame Tussaud's Waxworks, as Rothwell and Hitchen and I moved to a flat above Alf Morris's newsagents shop in Eastbank Street. We were up at 5am delivering papers. The round took an hour and a half and our best customers were the Brunswick Hotel and the Palace Hotel in Birkdale.

In 1951 I married my wife, Sheila, who came into the business along with Jack's wife. Mr Ball of Ball & Percivals found us a flat in Coronation Walk on the second floor above an amusement arcade and the Betty Bersi Dancing School.

In 1955, I branched out on my own when I took over the news kiosk in the old Ribble Bus Station, formerly the Cheshire Lines railway station. Sheila and I moved to Richmond Road. I was at the bus station for twelve years and then, in 1966, Mr Wood, who owned Mornington Road Garage, offered to sell me his newsagents business in Hoghton Street known as Smithies.

It was a little goldmine but after twelve months, Retail Price Maintenance finished and Moors Market next door opened their own kiosk selling cut-price cigarettes. I had been turning over a quarter of a million cigs a month and my takings plummeted. In the end, I had to knock 2d off a packet of twenty but I had the biggest range in town, over 50 different brands of both cigarettes and tobacco, and the customers came back.

It was a great business and we ran it for21 years until I retired in 1987. I met people from all over the world and taught myself how to greet them in 47 different languages.

At this point, Trevor treated me to a few of his multi-lingual salutations. I was very impressed. With his geniality, he would have made a great ambassador.

JOHN JAMES

John James, who was born in Port Talbot on December 10th 1932, became Southport's most successful club owner when he opened the Kingsway Casino in 1962.

I used to book groups into the Kinsgway in the sixties at a time when the country's top pop stars appeared there but I had never met John James in person until I visited him in his high-rise apartment in Lord Street one morning in May 2006 by which time he was long retired. Puffing on his pipe and sipping a glass of wine, he told me about his remarkable life.

I actually first came to Southport when I was six or seven. My dad had business in Manchester and we stayed in a flat for a short while in Scarisbrick New Road. It was many years before I came back.

I left school at fifteen and went to sea for eight years. I came from a showbiz background in that my great grandfather was one of the pioneers who built Blackpool Tower and my father was an entrepreneur who opened the first gambling casino in Britain, in 1959 in Port Talbot. The second, in Cardiff, followed a year later. He bought the equipment, the roulette wheels, from a firm called Joast in Paris, reckoned to be the finest made. When Leonard Jackson, who owned racetracks and was done for share-pushing, they call it insider dealing now, opened a casino in Glasgow, we supplied the equipment for it.

After Scotland, we moved into London. We took over the Contessa Club in Soho from two Pakistanis and, tying the name in with the popular comedian of the time, we reopened it as the Charlie Chester Club. It became a very well known venue in Sixties Soho with many famous, and infamous, faces passing through the doors. We had 24 hours a day gambling and it was a success from day one.

With such success elsewhere, why did John choose Southport for his next venture, a town full of retired people that had a reputation in the fifties of being 'a cemetery without walls'.

I knew there was a demand for a casino in the North West. The Isle of Man had one but you had to cross the water to get there. Southport was a seaside resort and at night was packed full of young people looking for fun.

We were told that the Kingsway Café on the Promenade might be up for sale so I came to look at it. Joe Ruane was already running a beat club there on the top two floors but I could see it had the potential to make a great casino. I bought it from Mrs. Ormerod whose mother, known as Rabbit Lucy, built it as a café.

I knew I would have to leave Port Talbot to run it. Dad wasn't keen on me leaving, he liked to have the family round him, but my mother persuaded him to let me go. By this time, I was married to my first wife and we had four children. I bought a house at 82 Scarisbrick New Road and we moved in in 1962. Two millionaires had lived there before me and I always regarded it as a very lucky and happy home.

Carl Young was the designer and architect whom I used to transform the Kingsway and the work was carried out by a Southport firm who did a superb job. We had a grand civic opening and the town's first 2am liquor licence was granted to us although it only came through the very afternoon of the opening day. Ronnie Appleby, who had worked there with Joe Ruane, became my manager and Mark Peters was my DJ/Compére.

We had cabaret, a restaurant and bars on the ground floor, a casino on the first floor and dancing in the Starlite Room on the second floor. I booked my cabaret acts through Bertie Green from London's Astor Club.

It was the most incredible club Southport had ever seen. We put on all the top entertainers of the time such as Tom Jones and Englebert Humperdinck and in the summer, when the British acts were doing summer seasons, we brought in American stars like Brenda Lee and The New Christy Minstrels.

After seeing the Kingsway successfully established, John had the idea of opening a second venue in the town.

I'd heard the Grand Cinema on Lord Street might be for sale so I went along one afternoon to see 'Sound of Music' and check the place out. As I was admiring the splendid building, and it was splendid, I got talking to the lady who owned it, a Mrs. Wood. She told me her late husband had owned nine cinemas at one time and the Grand, which her husband had had built as a special present for her, was the last one left.

The problem was the major circuits like Rank and ABC who kept all the best films for their own cinemas leaving independent operators like herself with re-runs and second rate films.

She wouldn't discuss money with me, I had to deal with her lawyers who were Brighouses, coincidentally my own lawyers too. I was told she'd turned down offers of over £100,000 but, in the end, I was able to buy it for £78,000 to be paid over three years. I think she sold it to me because she had heard I had given Easter Eggs and a donation to orphaned children in Formby.

Whatever goes round, comes round.

The Grand needed very little work on it. We offered free bingo but, to get to it, the people had to walk through the foyer that I'd filled with over two hundred slot machines. The organ pipes were still intact so I bought back the original organ and the Grand had music once again. Upstairs was the casino and we had a bar where the old kitchens were. From the start it was a great success

I went on to buy some betting shops, old Southport firms like Rimmer's and Bernard Litwack's. I built an amusement arcade at the back of the Kingsway and at one time I had over 1000 people working for me. I was one of the town's biggest employers.

I also gave a lot to charity. I sponsored an annual cup at the Flower Show, together with a £1000 donation and bought new instruments for the sea cadets. I equipped a local road cycling team and, of course, there were the children at the Formby convent.

By this time, I'd moved into Birkdale to a house called Merrilocks in Selworthy Road I kept a Piper Twin Commanche plane at Woodvale Aerodrome which I piloted myself down to Heathrow twice a week to attend to my London interests.

I was the first person after the War to open a casino on an ocean liner, first on the Empress of Canada then on the Empress of Britain.

I bought the Victoria Hotel on the corner of Neville Street and the Promenade. At the time, the hotels in the town like the Queens and the Royal and the Prince of Wales were becoming a bit run-down. Investors didn't see the potential in the town and I couldn't get the finance to renovate it. I had brilliant plans to turn it into a luxury hotel, casino and leisure centre but, in the end, I sold it to Maritime Housing who knocked it down to build flats.

The demolition of such a fine building as the Victoria Hotel, to be replaced by something totally out of character for the surrounding area, was one of the town's many planning blunders of the late twentieth century.

I would like to think it couldn't happen today but, despite all the civic societies, heritage committees, listed buildings and conservation areas, the Palace Cinema was recently razed to the ground so one shouldn't be too optimistic. Money talks. It wouldn't surprise me to read that Tescos were planning to build another superstore on the site of the Town Hall, Arts Centre and Library.

But to get back to John James! In the mid-60's, a potentially devastating change in the law threatened to close John's Southport operations.

Sir Stanley Raymond had taken over the Gaming Board and he decided that the number of cities and towns allowed to operate casinos in Britain was

to be limited to 28. Southport was not on the list.

We couldn't believe it. Blackpool had got a licence, fair enough, but so had St. Annes on its doorstep! Not to mention Liverpool and Manchester. Southport was a seaside resort with two thriving casinos and we didn't get one.

The night it happened, the mayor and his wife were in the club on a social night out to see Joan Regan, one of their favourite singers. I told the mayor what had happened and he asked me to call at the Mayor's Parlour in the morning. I went along and he told me to organise a petition and he would lobby politicians. Thousands signed and eventually the Gaming Board announced they were creating four extra licences. They couldn't very well just grant one. The four were Aberdeen (because of the gas industry), the Isle of Wight, Luton and....Southport.

A further snag came some time later when the Government changed the way casinos were taxed, basing it on the rateable value.

I called in some top-brass Manchester lawyers and argued that the casino, property and entertainment should be split into separate entities for . We won our case so we made a separate entrance to the casino at the Kingsway and Grand and thus paid £500 tax instead of £50,000.

In 1972, John sold his Southport businesses to Mr. Gasda and Mr. Karani, and moved, first to Jersey and then, in 1974, to Florida where he remarried a year later. When the marriage broke up in 1992, he returned alone to Southport and bought an apartment in the town centre. It wasn't long before he was back in business.

I took a lease on the downstairs bar at the Arts Centre and opened up as JJ's with a restaurant and live music every night. We opened 10pm-2am but it never really made any money and I got rid of it within five years.

I also got the licence for the boats and café on the Marine Lake. I bought twelve acres of land at the north end of the lake and had plans passed for a leisure centre and housing but, in that very year, the sea wall was breached and the council wanted a million pounds to mend it before any building work could be done. It was the days before European money came in. I managed to sell a portion off to the Winged Fellowship Trust who built a holiday centre for disabled people and I then disposed of the rest.

John still lives in his luxury apartment overlooking the town centre but at 74, he is in poor health. This he attributes to a life of 'burning the candle at both ends and in the middle'. I couldn't argue with that.

KEITH JERRAM

Keith Jerram was born in Southport in 1933. For many years he ran the family business, W.H. Jerram Limited, which had the distinction of being the largest firm of bookmakers in Southport. In 1988 he sold out to Ladbrokes and took early retirement. He lives near the town centre with his wife Nola.

In my early twenties, I used to go into one of Jerram's shops to place my annual bets on the Grand National and Cheltenham Gold Cup and it was usually Keith or his brother Colin who would take my money. I rarely got any back.

Nowadays, I just have a bet at the start of the football season for Southport F.C. to win promotion from whatever league they happen to be in that year. It's paid off three times in the last thirteen years which, at an average of 9-1 odds, puts me in front of the game, but now it's Ladbrokes who stand the loss, not Jerram's.

Over tea and biscuits at his home in 2005, Keith told me how the business first started.

My father ran a grocery shop in Clarence Road, Birkdale. One day, a customer came in complaining that his local bookie wouldn't take his bet. My father asked him what the odds were and, when told, offered to take the bet on himself. And that was the start of it all. There weren't many bookies around then. I can only remember Tommy Rimmer and Makins.

In 1939, we moved to Cypress Road and turned the front room into an office. In those days, you were only allowed to accept bets over the telephone. My dad canvassed for 'runners' to go round the factories and pubs taking bets from the workers. At one time he had over 50 men working as far away as Preston bringing back 'clockbacks' where the time was stamped on the betting slip to ensure the race had not been run. We paid the runners a shilling in the pound commission so it was in their interests to collect as many bets as possible.

As well as horse racing, we accepted bets on football. We paid £250 for the three highest scores and £130 for the three lowest. In those days, if someone won outright they had enough to put a sizeable deposit on a house. We made up our own coupons, which were printed by Crompton and Little in Linaker Street.

Keith came into the business in 1948 when he left Meols Cop School at the age of 14, served two years National Service in the RAF, and took over the running of the business in 1957 by which time his father had acquired an office in Adelphi Chambers in Hoghton Street.

The big change came in 1962 when betting was legalised. We moved the business from Cypress Road and bought a snack bar in Bispham Road, which became our first betting shop. Bedford Road followed in 1966. My younger brother, Colin, had come into the business in 1963 at the age of 22 and he took over the running of Bedford Road.

In 1968, we paid £2000 for premises in Tulketh Street next door to a coal yard, but the area was redeveloped in 1972. We sold out to International Stores who built a store on the site that later became Morrisons and now Waitrose. It was 1975 before we were able to find new premises in that street when we bought the old lock and key shop for £12,000.

We expanded out to Formby in 1970, taking over Peter Arcari's betting shop by the Blundell Arms (now the Cross House Inn) but that was only rented so we bought an old cottage opposite the police station in Church Road and turned that into the Formby shop. It's now a solarium.

Ainsdale followed a year later, another of Arcari's shops, but we moved within a few months, taking over a toyshop in Station Road, again because we wanted the freehold.

The last acquisition was in 1973 when we took over the old Co-op shop at the corner of Sussex Road and Windsor Road. Of course, only men were allowed in betting shops in those days. No women.

William Jerram died in 1980, aged 72. Keith continued to run the business for another eight years until Ladbrokes made him an offer for all the shops and he decided to retire.

Things had changed a lot in the years since Dad died. The multiples like Stanley, Coral and Ladbrokes were moving into every town but there is still a place for the local bookie. If he sets the odds right there is no reason why he shouldn't do just as well as the big boys .Of course, the rise in internet betting will affect business in the shops as more people use the Internet. In 1984, they brought televisions into betting shops. Before that we had loudspeakers broadcasting results via the exchange telegraph. Dog racing came in in the early eighties. Night racing had been going since 1976. We did well with betting on snooker but we never touched boxing.

Was that because boxing had the reputation for match fixing?

Not really. There was more skulduggery in horse racing and, believe it or not, in snooker.

Did you have any significant losses?

All bookies have those. We lost £50,000 when Willie Thorne won the Mercantile Cup as a 50-1 outsider. And a bloke came into Ainsdale shop with a Yankee. Twice he asked us to change one of the horses, which we did, and he ended up walking out with £12,000.

What about when Red Rum won the Grand National for the first time?

It seemed like everyone in Southport had money on Red Rum because he was a local horse but nobody really expected him to win. That race led to a lot of local bookies closing down. We lost a quarter of a million in today's money. We didn't hedge. I never believed in laying off bets. The trick is to set the odds right according to the starting price.

What is the most important attribute to be a successful bookie?

Always make sure you have enough money to pay out if the worst possible scenario happens.

OCCASIONS

Search for a Star hosted by Connie Creighton at the Floral Hall   Photo courtesy of Phil King

Birkdale Civic Society members with award from the Royal Anniversary Trust at St James's Palace London, 1992 (Ralph Gregson holding the award) Back Row far right Matthew Banks Consservative MP for Southport   Photo courtesy of Mike Braham

The original staff of Southport's first local radio station - Dune FM, 1997

Photo courtesy of Steve Dickson

Matrons & Staff at the Promenade Hospital, Circa 1963   Photo courtesy of Jean Woods

OCCASIONS

Mayor Sidney Hepworth meets 50's singing star David Whitfield Photo courtesy of Joe Ruane

Harry Fosters team, Southport Rugby Club, inspected by the Mayor Mae Bamber
1957-58 season.   Photo courtesy of Harry Foster

OCCASIONS

V.E. Celebrations in Mosley St, Harry Foster pictured as a young boy.

Photo courtesy of Harry Foster

elen Fjercoft, David Parry, Michael Braham, Ronnie Fearn   Tony Limont   ?   (Back row)
(Bootle)   (Ormskirk)   (Huyton)   (Southport)   (Wavertree)

Cyril Smith M.P.   Jeremy Thorpe M.P.   (front)

Mike Braham and a group of Liberals

Photo courtesy of Mike Braham

RAILWAYS

Woodvale Sidings - Old Cheshire Lines Railway

Photo courtesy of Harry Foster

Painting of bridge by Woodvale Station. Track follows the coastal road to Southport

Photo courtesy of Dave Rylands

Churchtown Station on the Southport to Preston line

Photo courtesy of Ron Ellis

Bridge over Bibby Road on Southport to Preston line

Photo courtesy of Ron Ellis

Ainsdale Station

Photo courtesy of Ron Ellis

Electric train leaving Hesketh Park Station

Photo courtesy of Charles Preston

DEMOLISHED BUILDINGS

King George V Grammar School,
Scarisbrick New Road

Photo courtesy of Ron Ellis

Victoria Hotel, Promenade and Neville St
corner

Photo courtesy of Harry Foster

Richmond Hotel, Scarisbrick New Road

Photo courtesy of Ron Ellis

Once Moors Market, later Cassidys, in
Hoghton St

Photo courtesy of Ron Ellis

The weighbridge at the Palace Hotel
Birkdale

Photo courtesy of Harry Foster

Off licence, corner of Duke St and
Shakespear St

Photo courtesy of Harry Foster

ENTERTAINMENT PLACES

Toad Hall, Ainsdale

Photo courtesy of Roy Adams

Scala Theatre (originally part of the old Winter Gardens Complex)

Photo courtesy of Jean Alexander

SOUTHPORT BUSES IN THE 1950's – Photos by Ron Ellis

Lord Street, Daimler bus

In St. James St, Leyland No 41

Outside the Shakespeare Hotel. Note the man parking a handcart on the far left.
Leyland Bus

Leyland No 30

Lord Street, Daimler bus

THEATRE

The SDC, SAOS, Maghull OS, Ormskirk OS & DC and Sefton TC 'Six of the Best' 2000

This photo reproduced by kind permission of Neil Hickson - Photographer (01704 822378)

Birkdale Congregational Church Drama Group, Circa 1952

Photo courtesy of Diana Barrington-Moss

ENTERTAINERS

Edwin Harper and Broadcasting Orchestra played for many years at the Floral Hall

Photo courtesy of Phil King

The world-famous VVercoe the Clown aka Arthur Pedlar

Photo courtesy of Arthur Pedlar

Southport singer Kingsize Taylor who had Crown Butchers corner of Liverpool Road and Halsall Road

Photo courtesy of Ron Ellis

Pete Jones & Maria Woods. Pete was resident singer for many years at the Scarisbrick Hotel and Maria told fortunes in Scarisbrick Avenue in 'Predictions'

Photo courtesy of Ron Ellis

'The Two Ronnies' Ronnie Fearn & Ron Ellis on stage at the Floral Hall for a '60's Reunion Night'Birkdale, August 19080's

Photo courtesy of Sue Ellis

Southport Community Radio supremo Jon Jessup in the station's studio in Birkdale, August 2006

Photo courtesy of Ron Ellis

SOUTHPORT CHURCHES

St Lukes Church

Photo courtesy of Geoff Ellis

All Saints, corner of Queens Rd and Park Rd, burned down

Photo courtesy of Geoff Ellis

Internor of Holy Family (wedding of Des & Sheila Walsh)

Photo courtesy of Sheila Walsh

Right: Interior of St Andrews (wedding of Tony & Janet Brothwell)

Photo courtesy of Tony Brothwell

Arnside Rd Synagogue

Photo courtesy of Mike Brahram

Choir at St Mary's Church, Carr Lane

Photo courtesy of Tony Brothwell

TIM TIMMERMAN

Mellors shop on Lord St, 1857 (then Dean's)
Photo courtesy of Tim Timmerman

Mellors on Lord St, 1950
Photo courtesy of Tim Timmerman

Invoice for goods supplied by Mellors, 1894
Photo courtesy of Tim Timmerman

Tim Timmerman's 'Dutch Chef' Cafe, previously Longs Elsinore Cafe, at 405 Lord St
Photo courtesy of Tim Timmerman

Baker's Meeting
Photo courtesy of Tim Timmerman

The Royal Clifton Hotel from across the Marine Lake
Photo courtesy of Ron Ellis

JEAN JESSUP

One of Southport's most notable personalities, Jean Jessup was born at 57 Pitt Street, Southport in 1923. She was a Conservative councillor for 33 years, representing Park and Cambridge Wards, and was twice Mayor of Sefton. She rates her greatest achievement in politics as winning the fight to save the Promenade Hospital building.

I knew Jean, socially, from the whist drives that she used to run in Marshside and now I was back at Marshside at the house where Jean has spent most of her life.

I went to All Souls School, which became Norwood Road in the 30's when the council took it over from the church. Mr. Rimmer was the headmaster. At 11, I moved to the High School, which was then housed in a red brick building on the corner of Scarisbrick New Road and Sefton Street, The headmistress was Mrs Diamond. Miss Ezard came later. We sported Panama hats in the summer and, no matter how warm September was, we had to wear long black stockings, gloves and velour hats in the winter terms. When we arrived at school each morning, we had to change into house shoes.

I left in 1939 when I was 16 to go to the Technical College where I took a senior secretarial course. My first job was secretary to Major Haynes who ran the Floral Hall Complex. My social life centred round All Souls. They had a youth club, girl guides, dances, usually with a 3 or 5-piece band, lifeboys (before the Boys Brigade days) and whist drives.

We used to go to the Miramar Café at the corner of Waverley and Lord Street. That was the place to go in the late 1930's. I wore gloves from Formstone and Cotteralls on Lord Street who sold hosiery and gloves. Very stylish.

I also joined the Young Liberals who met at the Gladstone Liberal Club at the corner of Poplar Street and Sussex Road.

Jean trained as a meteorologist in the WRAF during the War. In 1944 she married Cliff whose grandfather had been Mayor of Churchtown and had built many of the houses in Bankfield Lane. He was known as 'Caddy' Wareing and Jean became known locally as 'Caddy's Maggie's lad's wife'.

She returned to Southport in 1947.

Our first home was a corporation house in The Causeway, Crossens which was a new house on what had been farmland

In 1953, I started work in the offices at Robinsons on Lord Street, owned by Alderman. Aveling. He was one of the people who got the Flower Show going and he used to give free tickets to the staff every year. Nobody was allowed holiday leave on Flower Show week.

We sold curtains, linen and materials and we had our own workrooms. Miss Bather was in charge of lingerie, which included whalebone corsets and combinations. She wouldn't shake hands with commercial travellers as 'you didn't know where their hands had been'. Ellwalds Fabrics then bought the shop but business declined and they closed down in 1960.

Jean then went to work in the office of Excelsior Fireworks in Crowland Street . The fireworks were made in separate little huts overlooking the Old Links Golf Course. This was to limit the damage in case of fire. In fact, there were two big explosions when Jean worked there. The last one closed the factory in 1965.

The firm was run by the Bradley brothers, Fred and Edgar. Edgar was a Liberal councillor in the Lib-Lab coalition. Excelsior were the first people in the UK to manufacture Party Poppers and they made aquatic fireworks for displays on Fairhaven Lake in St. Annes.

When they closed down, I went to work as secretary to Simms Mitchell at the Forge Printing Works in Queen Anne Street. Simms became Mayor at the time and I looked after the books when his wife, Betty, was busy with her duties as Mayoress.

By this time, Jean herself had entered politics. Cliff's aunt, Mrs. Bancroft, had formed a committee to run Park Ward back in 1947. Jean put up as Conservative candidate in 1964 and won the seat from the Liberals by just 90 votes. Jean held the seat until she retired in 1997, after being beaten by Lib-Dem candidate Alexandra Farley, daughter of Dr. Tom Farley. In 1974, Park and Marine Wards were combined to make Cambridge Ward.

I was the first Chairman of the new Sefton Council in 1974 and I was upgraded to Mayor when Southport achieved borough status in April 1975. In 1985, I served a second term. Cliff was my consort on both occasions.

Our paths crossed again when Jean was on the Sefton Council Planning Committee. I owned a house in Lathom Road and I'd applied to turn the cellars into flats. The committee turned the application down. Jean blamed the delegates from 'the South' who had arrived in a luxury coach to inspect the property. I appealed and the Dept. of the Environment sent up a man from

Bristol. I walked him round the block and showed him how the cellars in just about every other house in the area were being used as living accommodation. I won the appeal.

Jean's greatest disappointment in politics was the failure to save the old Victoria Hotel at the corner of Neville Street and the Promenade.

The owners had applied for a subsidy that was being offered by the government at the time, so much money for every new hotel bedroom built. They were going to rebuild in the same style but, for various reasons, the work was delayed. They missed the deadline and went out of business. Someone else bought the site and built the modern Maritime flats, totally out of keeping with the architecture in the area.

As she seemed so keen on preservation, I asked her why Brian Naylor's plan to cover the Sea Bathing Lake back in 1971 had not been adopted by the council.

It was a nice idea but the condition of the building was too far gone by that time to make it viable. But it would certainly have looked better than the buildings that are there now, which belong more on a retail or industrial park.

'But think of the business rates the council are collecting,' I said and Jean smiled enigmatically. In these material times, everything comes down to money in the end.

In late 2005, Jean and Cliff moved to Lincolnshire to be near their grandchildren and, sadly, she passed away in 2006 before this book was published.

PHIL KING

Phil King was Southport's Director of Tourism & Attractions from 1977 to 1998. He is an Honorary Fellow of the British Resorts Association and was Chairman of their Advisory Committee for nine years. Phil was born on October 23rd 1939 in Ilkley and brought up in Hull.

Phil King is first and foremost a showman. I first ran into him in 1978 when I ran a dance for Southport FC in the Midnight Lounge. Some of the audience became a trifle overheated when they realised that the dancer was topless, something I had neglected to mention in the advertising. The Sunday Mirror ran the story, lots of publicity for the club and Phil and I have got on well ever since.

In the spring of 2006, Phil told me his story over a pot of tea in the lounge of the Prince of Wales Hotel.

I started out as a hi-de-hi man in Warner's holiday camps on the East Coast before moving into local government on the tourism side, at the Royal Burgh of Ayr and then at Barry Borough Council before I came to Southport.

Ralph Gregson was Chairman of the Tourism & Attractions Committee and we got on very well. The council encouraged me to take a lower subsidy on the Southport Theatre complex as there was a deficit after the previous administration.

The Tourism & Attractions Dept was responsible for not only the Floral Hall and Theatre Complex but also the beach, the Sea Bathing Lake and Pleasureland.

Southport beach was a tremendous money-spinner. When I first came, the Merseyside Motorcycle Club had races on the beach and the Motorcross events attracted big crowds. There was even an attempt on the Land Speed Record in the 1980's with a man wearing skis riding on the top of a car. They'd had a steamroller flattening the sand in advance.

The pleasure flights originated by Norman Giroux back in 1920 were very popular, with the Tiger Moth plane a familiar sight but the landing strip became silted up and the Civil Aviation Authority declassified it in 2001.

The lifeguard service used the famous DUKW vehicles to save lives and control the beach.

But the largest income came from car parking on the beach. On a Bank Holiday or weekend, we could have 15,000 cars in on one day at £1 a time. The world's biggest car park. What council wouldn't give their eye-teeth for an income generator like that?

Nowadays, the Air Show brings in huge crowds, as many as 300,000 people watching it from various vantage points and all of them potentially spending money in the town.

Pleasureland was run by the local authority but the infrastructure needed constant expensive upkeep and there was not the money available to spend on new rides so they put it out to tender in the 1980's and Geoffrey Thompson, who owned Blackpool Pleasure Beach, was chosen to run the attraction. They've revolutionised the place, bringing in famous rides like The Traumatizer and refurbishing the existing attractions.

We had the Sea Bathing Lake when I came but it only brought in money for four months of the year, due to the English weather, which made it uneconomical. Furthermore, the base of the pool was cracked due to the ream water and the cost of repair was prohibitive. It had to go.

Building the sea wall, which was aided by the European Objective One money we received through being in Merseyside, brought enormous benefits. It enabled the Ocean Plaza development to be built and kept the coast road open fifty-two weeks a year.

But the mainstay of the department's portfolio is surely the Floral Hall complex, which includes the Southport Theatre and the Floral Hall Gardens.

The capacity of the Floral Hall is 1200, when used for dances, rising to 1800 for conferences with concert seating. The hall is a leading Conference and Exhibition centre, helped by the fact that it has its own catering facility. Most of the big national organisations have held conferences here from the Lib-Dems to the National Union of Railwaymen.

We have always attracted some of the biggest names in show business but the best night we ever had was in the 1980's when we had 1200 dancing to Joe Loss & His Orchestra in the Floral Hall, Connie Creighton in the Midnight Lounge, Ken Dodd with two sold out shows in the Theatre, and a wedding reception in the Restaurant.

The worst night was when Dustin Gee collapsed in the dressing room during his pantomime show with Les Dennis in 1986, and later died in Southport Infirmary.

At one time, we showed films in the theatre and we were the first cinema in town to show Willy Russell's 'Shirley Valentine' with Pauline Collins. There were queues right down Bold Street.

One night, we had 1800 members of the Royal Antediluvian Order of Buffalos and they drank us dry. We had to send out to the Scarisbrick Hotel and borrow some of their beer barrels to keep us going till 2am.

For years we had Kenny Evans & his Midnight Orange Disco playing heavy metal music at the weekends. We never had any trouble with heavy metal and punk audiences because we used to frisk them. It was the ordinary dances where there might be bother!

Phil had many memories of some of the stars who appeared at the theatre.

An American act, Captain & Tenille, asked for avocados in their hospitality bowl. You couldn't buy such exotic fruit in the shops in those days so we had to send someone to Liverpool fruit market for them; Joe Loss would always have a Dover sole to eat before a show; Jack Jones once brought his father, Alan, onstage to sing his Dad's hit, 'Donkey Serenade'; Tommy Cooper took three days to leave town after his performance; one U.S. group demanded £25,000 in cash and when Steve Farrow and I handed it over backstage at the end of their show, their agent had a revolver in his brief case;.

Joe Longthorne holds the record for the longest standing ovation. The audience applauded a for 25 minutes and so many flowers were thrown on to the stage, we distributed them to local old people's homes.

Some of the riders the artistes attached to their contracts caused us problems. James Last, for example, demanded every member of his orchestra be paid in deutschemarks, which meant the Director of Finance had to go out and buy them, hopefully at favourable rates. We also had to supply them all with a three-course meal.

One of my favourite memories is of the 76 U.S. Army Band playing 'St. Louis Blues' as they marched from the Fire Station to the Prince of Wales Hotel, taking the salute at the Monument on the way and giving a concert on the green in front of the hotel in aid of the Merseyside Army Benevolent Fund.

There was once a to-do when a Sunday newspaper got hold of the story that an appearance by the male exotic dancing group, The Chippendales, had upset the good people of Southport. I was on holiday when it happened but I got a phone call warning me I might be in trouble when I returned and, sure enough, the press were waiting at the airport. However, it turned out England footballer Bobby Charlton was on the same plane and it was him they were looking for. When I got back to the office, nobody said a word so I can only suppose that nobody in the town read that paper.

The Chippendales had difficulty finding accommodation in the town. The boys oiled their bodies for the stage show and the greasy make-up used to come off in the beds and indelibly stain the sheets. Word soon got round and no hotel wanted to take them.

I reminded Phil of the commotion caused when The Chippendales came to town in 1992. In that same week, their similarly sparsely-clad female counterparts, The L.A. Centrefolds, also appeared and several people wrote to the Southport Visiter fearing that men witnessing The L.A.'s 'lewd act' would leave the theatre in a state of high sexual excitement which might lead them to rape innocent women.

I immediately replied to the Visiter wondering why, if this were true, those woman who had seen The Chippendales show were not in a similar state and were even now roaming the streets sating their lust on helpless, unsuspecting men. Furthermore, as many, mainly elderly, men were apparently aroused by Mrs Thatcher, did this mean the BBC should refrain from televising Today in Parliament?

Phil was also involved in controversy when there was a claim that the tide was bringing in sewage on to the resort's beaches. He was filmed on television, paddling in the sea beside the Pier, with his trousers rolled up to show the public they had nothing to fear from bathing in the Southport water. I noticed, however, he was careful not to drink it.

Southport was the first resort to hold the 'Search for a Star' contest back in the 1970's and this has become a nationwide event with heats in resorts all over the country.

The Floral Hall Gardens hosted a lot of popular events. The Radio One Roadshow regularly visited, we had the Vintage Car festivals, outdoor speciality acts and, of course, the beauty queens. Red Rum had his 'Freedom of the Borough' ceremony in the Gardens.

We brought back the English Rose contest, which had been discontinued due to silly 'political correctness, and the children's' Rosebud contest and both were highly popular and continued to the end of my time there.

I should mention Charles Mitchell and his Organ who played regularly in the gardens for years.

Tommy Mann was running the Marine Lake, which was a highly successful operation and has continued to be so with subsequent concessionaires. The Lake has speedboats, the paddle steamer rides, Southport Sailing Club, the West Lancs Yacht Club, a ski club and various water sports.

We ran the Steam Excursions in conjunction with the Southport Visiter, running trains to Wigan and Manchester. The Flying Scotsman was one of the engines used.

In addition to all this, we produced our own guidebooks and literature and developed the new Tourist Information Office in Eastbank Street Square, designed by Martin Perry.

Surely, I said to Phil, Southport's trade suffers from the town being out on a limb whereas, at Blackpool, the motorway comes right into the centre. Phil blamed Hitler.

The advent of the Second World War put paid to the proposed Ormskirk by-pass and it never got revived. I would take you to task about Blackpool though. When the M65 was built, 300 guest houses closed down because people could get back home easily at night. Southport is less than a two-hour drive for 13 million people, which makes it ideally placed for day-trippers.

Phil retired in 1998 and is now, among many other things, working for the Conservative Party in Southport. He lives in Churchtown with his wife, Maureen. They have one daughter, Sarah.

RONNIE MALPAS

Master Chef, night club owner, children's entertainer and crooner, Ronnie Malpas was born in Stockport in 1927 and came to Southport in 1949 after leaving his job as head chef at the Douglas Bay Hotel in Onchan on the Isle of Man. He worked in all the town's major hotels and, in 1958, opened Southport's first teenage nightclub, the Mocambo in West Street, where many of the new Merseybeat groups used to congregate.

By the mid-seventies he had given up a notable career in catering to take to the stage as a magician and children's entertainer, a career he still pursues to this day.

Like many teenagers in Southport in the late 1950's, I used to go to the Mocambo Club in West Street to listen to the latest records on the jukebox. It was run by a little man called Ronnie Malpas who guarded the hatch at the entrance. You bought a coke and were allowed through the barrier to climb the stairs to a small room crammed with people. The noise was deafening. Lots of the customers were aspiring musicians and I think Ronnie saw himself as the Larry Parnes of Southport.

I first came to Southport in pursuit of my wife-to-be, Joan, whom I met when she was on holiday with her family in the Isle of Man and stayed at the hotel I was working at. Joan's family home in York Avenue had been a theatrical boarding house for years, playing host to stars like Sid James, Joe Loss, George Formby and Norman Evans. Freddie Garrity (of Freddie and The Dreamers) was a visitor and stayed to paint the ceiling. Her father was known as Aussie Bob and he was a real character. He used to build greenhouses in his back shed.

Joan worked for Ball & Percival and got me a job at the Prince of Wales Hotel as chef and assistant patisserie cook. I moved to the Brunswick, a Jewish hotel at the corner of Lord Street and Duke Street and a fine hotel in its day. I took over as head chef after the Polish head chef had a heart attack. After that I was head chef at the Scarisbrick and then the old Palace Hotel in Birkdale which was the finest hotel in town.

Ronnie was having no difficulty in getting employment but he had the urge to strike out on his own. He had noticed the number of teenagers (as young people were suddenly called) hanging around street corners and decided to open a café to cater for them.

I found this derelict greengrocer's shop at the Coronation Walk end of West Street. They gave me a ten-year lease at £5 a week. I did the whole place out by myself and called it The Mocambo after a place I'd heard of in New York. We served coffee, hamburgers, hot dogs and coke downstairs, there was no alcohol, and I put a jukebox on every floor including the cellar. It was like a rabbit warren upstairs and I eventually knocked through to the room above the fish and chip shop next door.

Every appliance was wired from the only electric socket in the place and there was no Gents toilet. The fellows had to relieve themselves in the car park outside.

Luckily, dysentery was not prevalent in England at the time.

It was the beginning of rock'n'roll and we got all these young musicians coming in who were starting out playing in groups. I built a stage out of old beer crates and we let them practice in the Mocambo. You could hardly move most nights, it used to get so packed. God knows what the kids got up to on that top floor.

But the most famous performers at the Mocambo were Rhythm and Blues Incorporated who became the first Southport group to have a hit record (A new version of Richard Berry's 'Louie Louie which reached No. 40 in the charts in 1964).

I could see R & B Inc had talent and I put them on regularly at the El Rio in Neville Street, which was my second club. I'd bought the lease of the first floor of the old Thorpe's Tavern but the venture never really took off. We had Johnny Kidd and The Pirates and Freddie Starr there but the Klic Klic in Stanley Street got most of the crowds. I started managing R &B Inc and got them some good gigs. They played at Paul McCartney's birthday party at the Kingsway but I didn't rate the singer and tried to get the lads to back a girl group I had called The Candys. They refused and we parted company. They went to Jim Turner's Arcade Variety Agency in Liverpool who got them a recording contract with Fontana.

Ready for a change, Ronnie returned to catering and January 1st 1966 found him back at the Palace Hotel for a memorable evening to celebrate the New Year and the hotel's centenary.

To commemorate the event, Ronnie made a special cake that weighed an incredible 3 cwt and was four feet wide and two feet deep. A church scene was engraved in the icing, a hundred illuminated candles lined the edges and in the middle was a 'lake' with live goldfish swimming in it.

A bugler and piper led the procession as the cake was wheeled into the dining room to the delight of the assembled guests.

Later that year, Ronnie was appointed head chef at the newly refurbished Shorrocks Hill Country Club in Formby, owned by a Mr. Armitage. With a swimming pool, sauna, riding stables and international restaurant, Shorrocks Hill was a prestigious venue and Ronnie soon gained a reputation as one of the best chefs in the North West. He had five chefs working under him.

Roy Adams, who took over the club at a later date, said Ronnie was one of only two chefs in the country at that time who was able to spit roast a whole ox.

But Ronnie had the wanderlust and his next move was to take over The Bakery Restaurant on Warbreck Moor. In 1970, he built himself a mobile hot dog stand, which he used to couple up to his car and drive up to sites in the Lake District.

I put the stand together in Daisy Walk off Tithebarn Road, but when we tried to get it down the entry, it was too wide. I had to saw it in half and drag it down in two pieces.

In May 1979, Ronnie got his first gig as Merlin the Wizard.

I'd always been interested in performing, ever since I was a little lad. I taught myself to play the trumpet and ukulele and I was doing magic tricks when I was twelve. I decided to put an act together.

Using various non-de-plumes such as Mervin Ross, Bertie Beecham, Ronnie Gage with Weedy (a puppet) and Uncle Merlin & his Budgie Circus, Ronnie took to the stage as a magician and a children's entertainer. But he still worked freelance as a chef in various kitchens round the town including a spell at the West End Club.

I did gigs all over the country including the holiday camps for Butlins and Pontins.

In 1991, Ronnie went out to Thailand and opened a fast food business and, later a restaurant, in Chiang Mai, the country's northern capital and second city to Bangkok. He called the restaurant, the Mocambo. It was not long, however, before he returned to performing.

In 1994, I had some expensive orchestral backing tapes made and started going out as a Frank Sinatra tribute act using the name Ronnie Gage though I still did the magic shows. I had a spot on the 'Search for a Star' talent contest at the Floral Hall and I had this hen in the act that drank a pint of beer on stage. It brought the house down.

Ronnie was looking a trifle weary at the time I interviewed him at his Birkdale home in December 2004 and, when he told me his schedule, I could understand why.

Yesterday morning, I did an hour's magic act at a school in Churchtown then I had twenty minutes to drive to Maghull to a school in Poverty Lane. No time for lunch when I'd finished there because I had to get across to the other side of Liverpool for three o'clock to do another show at a school off Menlove Avenue. Don't forget, I had all those heavy boxes of equipment to carry in and out. I was so shattered when I got home that I fell over. It's too much, you know, at my age. I was 77 last Tuesday.

Eighteen months later, Ronnie was still going strong when I met him in Birkdale Village, full of enthusiasm about his latest show.

I've got a whole new act now. I call it 'Tribute to the Legends'. I take off Robbie Williams, Tom Jones, Eric Clapton and The Bee-Gees.

With bookings lined up in Thailand for later in the year plus his local gigs, Ronnie shows no signs of retiring as he approaches eighty. I'm not entirely convinced about The Bee Gees though. Those high notes...

TOMMY MANN

Tommy Mann was born in Shaw, Lancashire on November 14th 1935. He came to Southport in 1960 and was in charge of the Marine Lake in the Seventies before he turned to politics.

Like a lot of people, I first knew of Tommy because of his involvement with the Marine Lake. However, by the time I met him for the first time, at his Hesketh Park home in January 2006, he had just been chosen to be the next Mayor of Sefton. What had happened in between? And how did he get to run the Lake anyway?

I worked with my father who ran a children's amusements in the Tower grounds at New Brighton which had a miniature railway that ran along the Promenade front. He also had the lease on the Marine Lake there.

In 1959, three aldermen from Southport Town Council came over and invited us to tender for the lease of Southport's Marine Lake. It was a narrow lake at that time but they were building a sea wall that would allow for new development including a coastal road constructed from landfill. They created new islands at the North end of the lake and planted sparta and marram grasses to bind the sand.

That October, they duly awarded a 23-year lease to Tommy Mann & Son (Southport) Ltd with myself, my late wife and my parents as directors. We purchased stock from the previous owners, rowing, sailing, motor boats and launches but much of it was old and in need of replacement. However, we had our own boat building company. We built for several local authorities and it was easy enough for us to build new boats for Southport. The lake was considered a safe boating area as the average depth was only about four feet.

In our first season in 1960, we took over nine 'nobby' style yachts with ballasted keels with pig iron to give stability in shallow water; an all-new fleet of 15 motorboats; clinker rowing boats and launches that seated 40 people. We charged three shillings (15 pence) for thirty minutes hire.

As well as the marine activities, the family opened a catering operation at the side of the lake. Tommy's mother ran the 'Marine Lake Buffet Bar' by the Pier, which boasted the slogan, 'The best cup of tea since leaving home'.

It was an outdoor café with the kitchens and the ticket office inside the building. We served small pots of tea and the customers would sit outside and admire the view across the lake.

It was the end of the Wakes Weeks era when people poured into the town by rail. We had a list of the holiday towns and dates so knew when to take on extra staff. We found the visitors liked to come back onto the Promenade after their evening meal in the guesthouses and hotels so we started keeping the boats running into the late evening. At the height of the season we would have as many as 16 on the staff but only 5 in the winter for maintenance.

Very few people owned their own boats in those days. There were only 10-12 private craft on the Lake in 1959. The West Lancs Yacht Club had their HQ in the Victoria Baths and kept their vessels by the boathouse below the Promenade. They were mainly Flying 10's designed by Uffa Fox, small boats with fixed keels. We instigated an annual licence fee of five guineas for private users, which was not too popular as they'd never had to pay before.

About this time, the Daily Mirror in collaboration with television D-I-Y man, Barry Bucknall', advertised a new concept in boat building. It was a plywood, do-it-yourself kit, with the joints reinforced by fibreglass resin bandages, that could be assembled by any reasonable handyman and it brought the cost of sailing within the reach of the man in the street. Called the 'Mirror Dinghy', it cost just £60, and was a tremendous success. We felt sailing should be a sport for families so we formed the Southport Sailing Club in 1960 with a logo of a shrimp on a sandy background to acknowledge the town's tradition of shrimping. We charged five shillings a year member ship to pay for buoys and flags, there being no electronic starts in those days.

An old building on the Promenade side of the lake had been used as a changing room with the only access up steps from the lake. There were no toilets and it had become derelict. We did it up and turned it into a bar which was known locally as Tommy Mann's Bar. At first there was access only by a rear staircase from the lake but later we built a door onto the Promenade. This became the headquarters of Southport Sailing Club but non-sailing members were allowed in also.

In 1962, the excavation of the lake took place and the area was extended towards the sea with the islands formed from resultant spoil. Thanks to the building of the sea wall, there was a large area of reclaimed land on the far side of the lake. It was basically beach with no drainage or services but, in 1966, the West Lancs.Yacht Club and Southport Sailing Club both applied to build clubhouses there. We needed this to gain affiliation to the Royal Yachting Association.

There was a dinghy parking area with 300 spaces alongside the new clubhouse. The building was opened in 1967 by Alderman Simms Mitchell. By then we had 694 members with an Enterprise fleet of 46, 67 GP 14's and 105 in the Handicap Fleet. Within five years we added an extension to the clubhouse. We could have 80-90 craft on the lake on a good day. KGV, Stanley and Merchant Taylor's schools all had boats on the lake. We converted the old bar into a members-only club called The Lakeside Sailing Club.

Tommy sold the company in 1982 and the building was later renamed The Lakeside Inn and earned the accolade of the 'Smallest Pub in Britain'.

Business on the lake was booming although when Crosby Boating Lake was opened in the 1970's they took business from the south end of the town. People from Liverpool saw no reason to drive the extra fifteen miles to Southport when there was a lake waiting for them in Crosby.

In 1982, with seven years left on the lease, Tommy sold out and he and his wife moved to Port Erin on the Isle of Man. However, they didn't settle on the island and returned to Southport in 1989. Still keen on sailing, Tommy bought an offshore motor sailer with a galley and four berths, which he kept on Liverpool's new marina.

In 1994, he started his political career.

Since my wife died, I hadn't been out very much. Some friends persuaded me to go down to the West Lancs Yacht Club and, after a few visits, I agreed to become a member. My first duty was to man the car park at the 24-hour yacht race and I got soaked to the skin in heavy rain. The mayor and civic dignitaries were in attendance and Councillor Tom Glover asked me to think about putting up for the council. After much deliberation, I decided to give it a go and the following year I stood for the Conservatives in Cambridge Ward. I was elected and I've represented them ever since. Most of the concerns from my constituents are about local issues like Housing Benefit problems, street lighting and the condition of the pavements, etc.

When I joined, they said it wouldn't take up too much of my time. They said maybe I'd serve on three committees. Within a year I was on thirteen! Altogether I've held ten offices and at the moment I'm on the board of the Merseyside Fire Authority and a governor of Stanley school,. I'm out nearly every night in connection with council business. There's no way I could do all this unless I was retired.

I ran into Tommy a few weeks after this interview at the Connell Court 30th Anniversary Garden Party. Connell Court is a Methodist rest home and my 93-year-old mother in law, Marjorie Hargreaves, is a resident there. Tommy looked very imposing in his chains and he and his partner, Jean Lilley, the Mayoress, looked like they were really enjoying themselves.

GINGER McCAIN

Trainer of the legendary racehorse, 'Red Rum', a record three times Grand National winner, Donald 'Ginger' McCain was born in Grove Street, Southport on Sept 21st 1930.

Although I hadn't met Ginger before my interview with him for this book, I have had some connection with his success. I was the DJ at Red Rum's 21st Birthday Party, which took place in a marquee in Parbold in May 1986. I was also behind the decks at the Bold Hotel in 1977, when Tommy Stack was the hero of the evening having ridden the horse to his third Grand National victory, and at Blackpool in October 1977 when Red Rum switched on the Illuminations.

However, it was not until June 2006 that I finally got the chance to chat with Ginger when I visited him at his home in the grounds of Cholmondeley Castle in Cheshire, surrounded by hens, guinea fowl, a cat, five dogs and a hundred horses.

I went to Bury Road School, then Farnborough Road, infants and juniors, and finally Birkdale Secondary Modern. But I left at thirteen and a half. The War had started and nobody bothered overmuch.

My father was on the railways then joined Marshall and Snelgroves as a despatch man. In the War, he was with Air Traffic Control at Yeovil. He used to keep racing pigeons at our house, 316 Liverpool Road near The Crown Hotel.

My grandfather, John Wright, drove a horse-drawn open float for the Cranshaw Brothers who owned a butchers business called Southport Provisions in Tulketh Street. They sold black pudding, bacon and brawn etc to the corner shops around town. I joined him driving a float for £1 a week. We used to change the horses at lunchtime.

I was in and out of jobs. I was a van lad at the Co-op in Hillside. Every driver had a van lad and there were 30 vans on the road.

Then I was a perch boy at the Garrick Theatre where Mum worked in the Circle Bar. My job was to sit above the stage working the arc lamps. I got twenty-five shillings (£1.25p.) a week. We used to get all the London shows like 'Rose Marie' before they went to the West End. On Saturday nights, the flats (scenery) were loaded onto wagons and four or five horses were used to carry them to the station.

One year, I worked on the boats on the Marine Lake in the summer and I had a spell at a fox farm in Ainsdale. They used to breed them for the skins, fox furs being very fashionable at the time. For a short time, I became an apprentice baker at Jolley's Café on Lord Street.

When I was sixteen, I got a motor bike and used to race on the sands and at Altcar Rifle Range. George Leigh used to race with me. He went on to open a successful bike shop in Eastbank Street.

During the War, I was caddying at Hillside Golf Club when a Spitfire crashed onto the course. What is now Toad Hall was Queen Charlotte's Gunnery School and the Sands at Ainsdale housed the Wrens.

I was called up in 1948 to do my National Service and I became a despatch rider in the RASC. I was demobbed in the middle of summer in 1950 and got a job within three days. It was at the Southport Wallet Company in Cross Street but I only lasted four weeks. I couldn't stand being stuck inside all day.

So where do the horses come in?

I'd always been involved with horses because, in my childhood, they were all around you. Milkman used them, cabbies, rag and bone men, coal merchants, lots of local tradesmen like Bebingtons Bread in Hall Street, not forgetting the riding schools. I schooled horses for a Mr. Rabinowitz who dealt in horses and cattle. He was the forerunner of the car dealer.

Frank Speakman owned a sweet business in Southport. He was an ex-councillor who kept racehorses behind his house in Eastbourne Road. He eventually moved to Tarporley to start his own yard, and, when I walked out of the wallet factory, he invited me to go and work for him for £3 a week plus my keep. I didn't need asking twice. Dick Francis used to ride for the stable.

I came back to Southport in 1952 and went to work for Frank Thwaites of Goulders who ran a private hire taxi service with eight or nine cars opposite Birkdale Station. The Palace Hotel used Goulders for all their guests and I had people like Frank Sinatra, Norman Wisdom and Margaret Rutherford in my cab.

I did a bit of boxing in those days, training at a gym over the Bold Hotel in Lord Street.Kath had worked at the Co-op too. When Goulder's packed in the taxis in 1954, Kath came into partnership with me and we bought two cars, one of them an Austin 12 from Goulders.

It was at Walsh's stable in that I met my future wife, Beryl Harris. She lived with her parents in Seabank Road and worked in the Borough Architects office. We got engaged on Grand National Day in 1959 and we were married on Grand National Day 1961 at St. John's Church in Birkdale. After the *ceremony, we naturally went on to Aintree to see Nicolaus Silver win the big race. We had the reception that night at the Palace Hotel. It cost £48 for thirty guests.*

When Kath Walsh decided to get out of the taxi business, Jeff Langhorne came in with me. He'd been head lad at the Tarporley stables but now owned a grocers shop in Southport. We bought three cars on H.P. and called ourselves Cutler' Cars after a racehorse we knew.

Beryl and I found a car showroom in Upper Aughton Road for sale with Ball & Percivals. It had once been a pet shop and had a flat above. We paid £2,500 helped by a loan from the Natwest Bank and started selling second hand cars.

I'd dabbled with a few horses and had acquired a permit to train but my first racehorse was San Lorenzo, which I kept in stables behind the Blundell Arms. It was time for me to get my full trainer's licence. I went on to buy the properties next to mine including an off-licence and brewery. I now had space for four cars but, more importantly, there were stables in the yard behind converted from what had once been a bottling factory.

But the turning point in Ginger's life came in August 1972 when he went to Doncaster sales to bid for a horse for one of his owners, Noel Le Mare, who asked him to find a mount that could be trained for the Grand National. Ginger paid £6,000 for a five-year-old gelding. His name was Red Rum.

The horse had had problems in the past with lameness but I took him out onto the beach to gallop. I knew that the shrimpers that I used to see as a lad would take these old crippled horses out to sea, dragging their carts behind them, yet after they had been in the sea for a time, they were transformed. Maybe it was the minerals in the sea water or maybe there was less stress on the joints walking through water, I don't know, but it certainly worked with Red.

Nowadays, the beach has become marshland to protect the natterjack toad which is ridiculous, especially as you never get natterjack toads on the beach anyway.

In 1973, Red Rum came from fifteen lengths behind to beat Crisp at the line and win the Grand National.

By this time, I had four lads working on the yard and just eight horses.

In 1974, Red Rum won the race for the second time. Local bookmaker, Stan Makin, thought there was no way a horse trained in the back streets of Southport could win twice so he stood all the bets instead of laying them off. He lost a fortune.

After coming second in the race in each of the next two years, Red Rum gained a famous third victory in 1977 with Tommy Stack on board.

John Craig held a party for him at the Bold Hotel on Lord Street and we brought the horse into the ballroom with half Southport trailing after him cheering and applauding. Later, John renamed the Carlton Hotel on Lord Street, which he also owned, The Red Rum Hotel.

Red Rum was entered for the National the following year but Ginger pulled him out at the last minute when the vet found a bone in his foot had a small fracture.

I didn't want the old boy to end up as a cripple or be shot. Instead, he became a celebrity. On the advice of a friend, we made him into a limited company to protect him from exploitation and he embarked on a string of personal appearances. They erected a statuette to him in the Wayfarers Arcade and a statue on Aintree Racecourse.

The racing part of Ginger's life was at its peak but the car business was sliding into bankruptcy.

I had a partner in the car business called Peter Cundy. We'd paid £30,000 to modernise the showroom and take on a new car dealership with Austin Rover which cost us £30,000. Ken Dodd performed the opening ceremony. The agency terms compelled us to buy a minimum number of new models with appropriate spare parts plus provide a fully equipped workshop and the whole thing proved to be a disaster as the money flowed out. I was on the verge of losing our home (Peter had cleverly put his in his wife's name without telling me) and I was only saved by a loan from my dear friend, Stan Markland. Peter left and I went back into the second hand car business with a salesman called Paul Nolan who now runs the business himself and leases the premises from me.

Despite the publicity Ginger had brought to Southport, he was starting to get a hard time from the council and, in 1990, the McCains left the town they loved.

I'd applied to extend the number of boxes in the yard but neighbours had started objecting to the noise form the stables. Southport had now come under the control of Sefton Council, having been joined with the rough neighbourhood of Bootle, a crazy decision. Busloads of councillors came to inspect us and rejected the application. Coupled with the fact that the increased traffic in the street was becoming a problem, we decided it was time to move on.

A dairy farm called Bankhouse on the Cholmondeley Estate near Tarporley had come on the market. It had 200 acres and was ideal for what we wanted, even thought the rent was £26,000 a year. We moved in that winter and have never looked back.

In October 1995, Red Rum died but, incredibly, Ginger's success story in the Grand National was not over.

I paid £75,000, the most I'd ever spent, for this Irish horse to try and win the National again, this time for John Halewood. It was called Amberleigh House and it did the trick in 2004, putting me alongside Fred Rimell as the only men to have trained four National winners.

My proudest moment was when I was awarded the Freedom of the Borough of Sefton in 2003.

Ginger has now handed over his trainer's licence to his son Donald but he is still active every day on the yard and still attends the horse sales. But, as he admitted to me, he greatly misses Southport and likes to get back to see the old place when he can.

KEITH MITCHELL

Keith Mitchell was born in Southport in 1944. His father was Alderman Simms Mitchell who was Mayor of Southport in 1967-8. Keith inherited the family printing business, Mitchell & Wright.

Our paths have crossed at various times over the years. In the Eighties, Keith was social secretary of the West Lancs Pony Club and I used to do the discos for their pony club dances. We are both vice presidents of Southport F.C. and Mitchell & Wright printed my second book of poems, 'Last of the Lake Poets'. Needless too say, they also print the Southport FC programmes too.

We sat in his office at Banastre Road, beneath a picture of Southport's 1998 Wembley side, and he told me first how the business had started.

My father, Simms Mitchell. He came to Southport in 1922 at the age of eleven when his family moved here from Lytham. Dad had an accident when he was seven when a piece of string he was playing with caught fire badly scarring his face but he never let it affect his life. He went to Christ Church School and originally worked for his father who was a carpet salesman

My father and Les Wright started the business in 1935 in Les's parents' washhouse in Claremont Road. When war broke out in 1939, Les left for Brockhouses, on Rufford Road Bridge where they made Vulcan cars whilst my father joined the RAF.

In 1946, back in harness, they opened a shop in Victoria House, Hoghton Street, later occupied by Bain & Faut Estate Agents, and set up as Mitchell and Wright Office Equipment. Two years later, they moved to 131a Eastbank Street, behind Murgatroyd's photographers and The London Tea Company, an old-style high-class grocer's. They now concentrated on the printing side of the business and were basically a letterpress operation with a workforce of ten.

In 1952, Dad bought a building in Queen Anne Street owned by Mr. Hewitson, the vet, who used to shoe horses on the ground floor and paint carriages upstairs, the carriages being hoisted up through a trap door. The place was called The Forge on the title deeds so it became The Forge Printing Works. They had one of the first Litho presses and by 1959 were the third biggest printers in Southport, behind Southport Printers at the Southport Visiter and West Lancs Press run by Geoffrey Binks.

In the meantime, of course, Simms was pursuing a parallel career in local politics.

Dad stood in the Talbot ward in 1937 as a Liberal but he later crossed over to the Conservatives. He went on to become an Alderman of the Borough and was Mayor of Southport in 1967-8. He rated his greatest successes as gaining planning permission for the Crematorium in 1952 and setting up the Centenary Teak Appeal, which placed seats all, round the town. He died in 1991 at the age of 79.

I went to school at Norwood Road, Stanley and the Technical College where 'Killer' Walsh was in charge.

I'd been going to St. Luke's Church since I was seven. I was an altar boy. It was very Anglo-Catholic, what they called a 'high church'. Tony Travis was head choirboy. When I was older, I started going to St. Luke's Youth Club in the church hall, which was run by Derek Edgar. This was in 1957. You became a senior member at 16 when you were allowed to play snooker and table tennis. We had a coffee bar in the cellar and ran record hops. At first we played the new-fangled 45's on a Dansette record player but it wasn't long before we started booking groups like The Teenbeats.

I played a lot of football, all through school and then 15 years as a full-back with Southport Trinity who played on The Rookery in Roe Lane.

I was only 22 when my father became mayor. I'd served my time, six years at Liverpool College of Print from 1960, so I went in to run the business in his absence. We moved to our current Banastre Road premises in 1988 where MB Colourprint used to be.

We are probably the biggest print operators in town. We have expanded from 20 to 30 workers with six multi-colour presses, specialise in any printed product up to B2 size and send work all over the country.

Although he has never followed in his father's footsteps politically, Keith has been a member of several organisations.

I was on the parish council in Parbold from 1885 to 1986. I joined Southport Round Table in 1968 and helped form the Southport Hesketh branch in 1976. I have been Chairman, Area Chairman and National Councillor of Table and also a member of Southport & Ainsdale Golf Club.

Keith now lives in Mawdesley with his wife, Nicky. They have two children, Gemma and Gill.

PETER & MARGARET MOLLOY

Peter Molloy was born in Southport in 1931. He runs the family furniture business from his shops in St. James Street and Lord Street. He is married to Margaret (nee Kershaw) and they have three sons and three grandsons who have followed them into the business.

I first ran into Peter in the early seventies when I started buying houses and turning them into flats. I used to go to the auctions for my furniture and carpets. Peter was always there buying stock for his shop and we were often bidding against one another for the same lots. More often than not, he would bid higher and win the sale. Days later, I would end up at his shop in desperate need of a bed or suite and he would sell me the one that we'd both bid for at the auction.

Margaret's sister, Pat Kershaw, was the first English Rose back in 1951. Had Margaret entered in 1952, she could easily have been the second.

At his shop in St. James Street, Peter told me how the family business had started years ago.

I was born in the flat above the shop in Ashley Road. My mother, Jenny Molloy used to take goods to Ormskirk Market on a horse and cart every Thursday and Saturday. The horse was kept in a stable behind the shops in Ashley Road.

Jenny used to buy lots of linen at house clearances. In those days, the thirties, you bought everything. Nowadays, people keep bits of things for themselves in case they are worth money. She boiled the linen in a dolly tub using a posser, a round copper instrument with holes in the side. She ironed the linen till it was like new. She was famous for her linen. It was a big part of her business. People used to come especially for it.

Jenny eventually opened the shop in Ashley Road which we still own today although the business closed in 1999.

My great-grandfather, Henry (Jack) Robinson, was a fisherman who manned the lifeboats. He was one of two men saved on the Eliza Fernley lifeboat when their boat went down in 1876 trying to rescue the crew of the German barque Mexico, which had gone aground off the coast at Ainsdale.

Peter went to school at St. Marie's in Seabank Road then on to St. Mary's in Crosby. When he left, he served five years as an apprentice coachbuilder before being called up. On leaving the forces in 1955, he joined the family business, working mainly on the vans for the first five years. .

We started the removals business during the War. We had the first removal van in Southport. Some days in the summer, it got so hot on the vans we took the doors off to give us some air. I drove under Peel Street Bridge one day and, coming back, the road surface must have been that bit higher and the bridge ripped the canvas roof off the van.

In the War years, we stored furniture in an old mill building in Ashley Road. We lived round the corner in Hall Street.

The Molloys bought the St. James Street premises in 1966 from a Mrs, Bond who was a furniture dealer. Jenny carried on in Ashley Road whilst Peter ran the new shop.

We started off with an empty shop. There was a place in Liverpool selling cottage suites for £12. We had to decide whether the red or the green would sell best as we couldn't afford to buy both. We had so little stock we used to put what we had in the window with a screen right behind it. As we accumulated more things, we moved the screen back. We bought both at auctions and privately, house clearances and the like.

Margaret had her part to play in the business.

We had a huge riveter machine. We'd buy tubes of this material that was vinyl on one side and stockingettes on the other. I'd cut it up and put a couple of rivets in and make shopping bags out of it. When I'd got a reasonable number, I'd put the children in the back of our old Morris Traveller and drive over to Blackpool and sell them to gift shops.

We used to go to the Potteries and buy up rows of unmatching china. When we got back home, we'd set them out on a trestle table and match as many up as we could and sell them in the shop. Half a crown for a matching cup and saucer. Any left over we'd hang on to and try to match them up with ones from the next trip.

Peter later opened another shop on the corner of Lord Street and Seabank Road selling only new furniture and gift items. Since then, the family have gone on to open shops in Lytham and Hoylake.

BRYAN NAYLOR

Bryan Naylor was born in Blackburn on June 16th 1929. He came to Southport in 1946 with his family and joined his father in his building trade contractors business. In 2002, he became one of the founder members of the Southport Party. He lives near Churchtown with his wife, June. They have two children and six grandchildren.

I interviewed Bryan in the garden of his home during the July heat wave of 2006. I'd never met him before and had I not known he was 77, I would have taken him to be in his early sixties. Obviously sea air and politics are a rejuvenating mixture.

When I was a teenager in Southport in the late forties, the place to go was the Floral Hall on a Saturday night. There was no bar, unless they had a special licence, and everyone used get a pass out to go across to the Queens Hotel in the interval to get a drink. Bands like Ted Heath, Vic Lewis, Nat Gonella and Ray Ellington used to play there and that's where I met my wife, June, who worked in Boots Circulating Library.

There was a lot going on in the town. The Temperance Hall in London Street ran dances as the Palais de Danse, Bill Gregson played the Scala on a Sunday afternoon with a 12-strong band and Mrs Batty used to play piano with a band in the old Leyland Arcade, now Wayfarers.

Our meeting places in the town were the Kardomah Café on Lord Street, Rossis ice cream parlour in Neville Street and Uncle Macs in Seabank Road. 'Pop' Reece opened the first Chinese restaurant in the town in the early fifties, the Oriental in Avondale Road, and used to hire Chinese cooks coming off the boats at Liverpool.

We used to go to the Sea Bathing Lake in the summer. It was always packed out. In 1971, I approached the council with plans for putting a glass dome over it to make it an indoor leisure centre but they weren't interested. Years later, Rhyl's Sea World and Center Parcs showed what a money-spinner it could have been. Now they are thinking of building something similar on a smaller scale called Splash World although at one time, they were going to use my name for it, the Aquadome.

Disappointed at the council's decision, Bryan built a giant swimming pool in the back garden of his Marshside home and, yes, he put a plastic dome over it and very impressive it looks over 30 years later.

When we dug up the garden to install the pond, we found driftwood and seashells only two feet deep showing the sea once covered this area, right up to the old Churchtown Station.

Bryan first became involved in politics in 1990 when he joined the Liberal Democrats and became a member of the Lib-Dem think tank. But, in 2000, disillusioned with what he saw as complacency of the main parties, he became a founder member of the Southport Party.

The party was founded by John Morris. There were nearly twenty people who were original members, all of whom were appalled by the way Sefton Council was ignoring Southport's problems in 2002. Especially as the old Southport Corporation had provided such a good service in the past when the town was an independent county borough. We determined to do something about it.

In the by-elections that year, we had prospective candidate in seven wards and three of them were elected. They were Margaret Brown in Meols Ward, David Cobham in Cambridge and James Grundy in Kew who knocked out the Lib-Dem leader, David Bamber. They campaigned on a platform of' Southport Out of Sefton' after 22 years of neglect and a 9% increase in council tax that year. Three out of seven for a new party was a tremendous feat and showed how disillusioned the voters had become with the old regime.

Although in 2006, the Southport Party no longer has a seat on the council, I feel our existence highlighted the shortcomings of the town and caused the other parties to treble their efforts until the council started to take notice to rectify them. A lot has been done over the last six years to improve standards in the town.

When you see the rejuvenated Pier now, one of the town's greatest attractions, and the magnificent new bridge, it is hard to believe that the Pier came within one vote of being demolished.

The Southport Party were behind the pedestrianisation of Chapel Street in principle but we always said there should be a trial run. Now it is too late to go back but we are currently pressing for a ring road linking Virginia Street with the Derby Road roundabout by ASDA, which we believe is urgently needed.

We also think it would be a good idea to have an annual event to celebrate Lord Street, a thoroughfare which inspired the creation of boulevards of Paris and Washington, and hope this suggestion might be taken up in the near future.

Bryan is also a member of two other important local groups.

I formed the Southport Beach Protection Group in 2000 with John Shawcroft. This was the beach that used to advertised as 'seven miles of golden sands. My wife used to walk along it from Formby to Southport as a girl and described it as a delightful walk. By the turn of the century, with the exception of Ainsdale, it was in dire condition, overgrown, covered in mud and full of nitrates from the river after years of sand removal.

Currently, we are proposing the possibility of privatising the administration and maintenance of Southport beaches and our aim is to stop sand removal within five years.

We are hampered by quangos like English Nature who have managed to stop the popular Hovercraft service to Blackpool on the grounds that is might disturb the birds. The same organisation is chopping down large chunks of the pinewoods to restore the natural sand dunes that are the habitat of the natterjack toad. I am involved with Sefton Coastwatch who are fighting this. When have toads been more important that humans?

I had to agree. On that basis, one could argue in favour of demolishing Ocean Plaza for the same ecological reasons although the council would lose a tidy sum in business rates so I fear the toads would be the loser there.

We have also been involved with the Hesketh Park Refurbishment having got the derelict toilets rebuilt and reopened, which is essential for the park's future.

I told Bryan that I thought a lot of the things he'd campaigned for had resulted in important benefits for Southport. 'I'm not figuring on being important,' he replied. 'I just want to do my best for this lovely town and campaign for improvements.'

ALEX PATON

Alexander Paton was born Southport on August 12th 1940. His father was one of the partners of F.W. Paton & Sons, Alex's grandfather's family painting and decorating business, based at 49 Claremont Road, the first dormer bungalow built in Birkdale. His mother owned a general store at 33 Everton Road.

Alex has been married to Elsie, a community nursing sister, for 42 years. They have two sons, James and Charles.

His C.V. reads like a sample of the town's employment scene over the last fifty years, showing the change from manufacturing to service orientated businesses.

When I was an agent in 1963, I used to book a group called The Toledos into local pubs and clubs. The club owners complained that they were too loud but they explained this by pointing out that they had to play loud to make themselves heard over frenzied thrashing of the drummer. That drummer was Alex Paton.

One afternoon in 2006, in the smoke-filled lounge of his bungalow in Crossens, which he has been extending for the past eleven years, he told me his life story over a dozen cigarettes and two coffees. Roy Castle would not have been amused.

My mother's shop was one of the first in Birkdale to sell Scott's Empire bread, baked in Aintree. She also managed to obtain a supply of biscuits from the Elkes & Fox factory in Burscough in the austere post-War days of Labour's Stafford Cripps and rationing, Crowds of people were queuing for them round the corner into Vaughan Road. Queuing was becoming a national pastime. When Marks & Spencer in Chapel Street received the first bananas after the War, the queue started down Corporation Street and went back round Christ Church, along Lord Street past the Trocadero Cinema and ended halfway down London Street.

Alex attended school at Linaker (Infants)/Sefton Street (Juniors) and Christ Church Secondary Modern but started his working life very early.

I was working as a van boy on Coulton's bread vans when I was eleven. The drivers used to pay us out of their own wages. I had two paper rounds.at newsagents in Eastbourne Road and Claremont Road.

At 14, I started work on the boat deck at Peter Pan's Pool at the weekend, bringing in the canoes, taking the money, putting on the records and touting for custom on the mike. Lots of students worked there. It was run by Maxwell, Manners and Pring, a Brighton company, and the general manager was Gerald Dawes known as 'Daddy'. He used to run the Union Jack up a flagpole every morning before opening the ground. It was like 'Hi De Hi' The most popular ride was the Speedway track. The lads who worked on it were nicknamed 'jumpers' because they used to jump onto the back of the speeding cars, risking life and limb to bring them in.

Throughout the late forties and fifties, Southport hummed like a dynamo. During the season, coaches and excursion trains brought in tens of thousands of day-trippers. It was a boom time for British seaside resorts.

In the Teddy Boy era there was little real violence. The last bus at 11pm cleared the town centre. People had to be up for work the next day.

At weekends in the fifties, crowds of teenagers congregated outside the National Westminster Bank and Alexanders at the corner of Lord Street and Neville Street.

Tommy's Rock Shop in Neville Street was popular with the teddy boys as it had wall-mounted pinball machines and a jukebox with all the latest hits on it for 2d. a go. Tommy stood in a gap beside the rock stand in his pork pie hat deciding who to let in and who to bar. His son-in-law was a taxi-driver and caricaturist and his drawings were displayed on the arcade walls.

Further up Neville Street, Major Lucas ran dodgem cars in his amusement arcade Later the premises were used for held mock auctions.

Len Smith, band leader, Co-op milkman and a gentleman, ran popular dances at the Temperance Hall in London Street. Later, a Mr. Fitton took over. He charged 6d on a Monday, 3d. on a Wednesday and 9d. on a Friday, and he banned all drape jackets and drainpipe trousers, the Teddy Boy's uniform. Bill Gregson's Band played every Sunday afternoon at the Scala.

There was also Rossis, Uncle Macs in Seabank Road and the Trocadero Milk Bar next to the cinema.

I left school at 15 and started an apprenticeship as a motor mechanic at Davies's Garage in Upper Aughton Road for 27/6d. a week; considerably less than I'd earned as a schoolboy. That only lasted 6 months and I went back to Coultons as an HGV repairs apprentice in the workshop. I stayed their five and a half years.

In 1961, I moved to ICT who occupied the old Brockhouse premises in Rufford Road. Mullard were in the other half of the factory moulding magnets for TV's. I was on the production line making early computers and tabulators, the 313 high-speed sorter and punch verifier, which worked on a Jaquard sensing system operating electronically through punched cards. ICT was paying London loading. Having finished my time, I was earning £12 a week, good money for Southport at that period. It wasn't to last. IBM cornered the market with punched tape and we were all made redundant.

ICT closed down in 1962, a year when Merseybeat was reaching its height. The era of trad jazz and skiffle was being supplanted by rock'n'roll. All over Britain, teenagers were making their own music and one of the centres of the movement was the North West. The Beatles and Merseybeat had a profound influence among many young people in the Southport area in the early Sixties. Many local budding musicians formed groups and quite often continued playing for the rest of their lives. Alex Paton was an aspiring drummer hoping to become a professional musician.

I bought my first drums, Ajax White Pearl, from Frank Hessy's in Liverpool for £250 on hire purchase in 1960, a hell of a lot of money then. I taught myself to play, with help from Joe Walsh. With Pete James (Vocals), Eric Wright (Rhythm), Ray Marshall (Lead) and Ian Sheldon (Roadie), we formed The Toledo Four. We practiced in West Ward Con Club, a wooden hut opposite Coulton's in Duke Street. Our first booking was a 21st birthday party at the Blundell Arms Hotel in Upper Aughton Road for £1.17.6d.

We started out, like most groups, playing youth clubs then moved on to weddings and engagements parties in church halls before graduating to beat clubs and night clubs. We played all the local venues like The Glenpark, The Klic Klic in Stanley Street, The Marine View (later the Kingsway), The Tropicana and Revel in Eastbank Street and the Scherazade in Stanley St. We also appeared on the Saturday morning shows at the Regal (ABC Minors) and Gaumont (GB) Cinemas where they let us practice before the doors were opened.

When I was made redundant from ICT, I went back to Coultons selling Sunblest bread in Kirkby for twelve months before eventually turning fully professional with the Mersey Four, Billy Abbott, Russell Peart, Eric Wrught and myself. We did the first of many Scottish tours in 1963 and we were also the first Southport group to tour the club circuit in Germany, as Tony Carlton's Mersey Boys, as well as playing all over the U.K..

But, although he continued drumming for the next 40 years, Alex soon found himself back in Southport embarking on an unusual variety of jobs.

My next job was making artificial hip joints at Latimers Engineering in Shakespeare Street. Within six months, I'd moved again, this time to English Electric on the East Lancs Road making switchgear. I had also started a residency at Skelmersdale Labour Club which was to last seven years.

I came back to Southport in 1968, fed up with engineering and was appointed manager of Budget Rent-a-Car, a franchise operation that had opened in Southport Engineering's car showrooms in King Street. They were an international company who had broken into the burgeoning car rental market, undercutting market leaders Hertz and Avis. They had 87 operations in the UK alone. I built up the fleet from 7 cars to 34 cars plus a number of vans.

Alex joined Hertz two years later, at their truck rental depot in Liverpool, but he found this unsuitable and it was not long before he was back in Southport as an assistant manager, first at Curry's in London Street followed by two years managing Lex Furnishings' Crosby branch. His next job was area manager designate at the Sleep Shop, a subsidiary of GKN, round the corner from the station in London Street, and he then moved on to be manager at Telefusion on Chapel Street. 1977 found him selling insurance for CIS based in Lord Street. By this time, he'd had more than enough of working for other people and decided to branch out on his own.

Trust House Fortes' Entam Division owned seven leisure centres on British piers. At Southport they used to hire out machines called 'Cyclo Mobiles' for day-trippers to ride around the Promenade. There were eighteen of them in all. Unfortunately, people rode them all round the town and quite often abandoned them in smashed condition in the most unlikely places. One was found one in a shed at the Technical College, a couple in the Marine Lake and even one at Woodvale. I was brought in to repair and renovate them. I had a workshop under the Pier and set up a spray booth where I turned a pile of scrap metal into serviceable machines.

However, this lasted only one season as the cycle business was sold on whereupon Alec turned his hand to property renovation, steel erection and painting and decorating before going back into running a business again.

I bought a couple of 30 cwt. vans and set up a transport company. We were trading well but when I started to expand, I couldn't get drivers of the right calibre. Also, our prime business was delivering plastic injection mouldings for toys and this fell away as more and more toys were fitted with computer chips. British toy manufacturing had all but collapsed.

I jacked it in and opened a second-hand shop in Sussex Road called The Tat Shop. At this time, I was still drumming at night at the Spectrum Rooms, Bootle and running the catering operation at Skelmersdale Labour Club.

When this finished, I teamed up with popular organist, Ronnie Hancock, and we played several residences like the Marine View at the Queens Hotel, the Dixieland Showbar, Toad Hall and the Marine Club.

He also started to do PR work on a consultancy basis for Silcocks Leisure Group.

The Silcock Family first brought a fair to Churchtown in the 1920's, on land rented from the Fleetwood Hesketh family. Over the years, they made annual visits to Blowick and the Isle of Wight Farm on Birkdale's Moss Road, travelling with traction engines. One of the big attractions after the War was Matt Moran's Shamrock Garden Boxing Booth and they had the Swirl, the Waltzer and a Noah's Ark.

As kids, we used to go to the Birkdale Fair at night and the sound of Frankie Laine, Johnny Ray and Guy Mitchell records blasting out over the roar of the dodgems was tremendous.

In the late 1950's Silcocks moved into Pleasureland with rides like the Swirl of Life, the Dodgems and the Octopus. In those days, Southport Corporation granted five-year leases and the fairground was under the control of the Publicity & Attractions Dept of Southport Corporation. Alderman Barber was the chairman and Councilors Bill Bellis and Bertie Dawson were on the committee.

Trust House Forte had got the Dixieland Showbar on the Pier Head where the old Pier Pavilion used to be. They had turned this into a nightclub and disco which they renamed Follies but in 1962 sold out to Silcocks.

I did the advertising, marketing and promotion for Follies and was eventually appointed General Manager. We put on discos and cabaret seven nights a week and it was very popular although it could get rough in there at times. We also had one of the largest functions rooms in town, rivalling the Floral Hall in capacity. We also staged fashion shows and conferences

Eventually, the owners realised their was more money in slot machines and arcade games and turned it into the Funland leisure complex, comprising a huge amusement arcade with bingo, a café and, outside on the forecourt, a hundred year old carousel, flagship of the company.

Alex's job was over but within a couple of months he was back in the entertainments industry, this time on the management side. With a partner, he opened the Northern Linden Entertainment Agency, operating from premises on Hart Street Bridge opposite the Blue Anchor pub.

We were one of the first agencies to build up a computer-booking database of musicians and acts. We had international contracts with the Hilton hotel group and many other major operators like Top Rank and THF. We even provided the entertainment for the Conway Tunnel Opening Gala Night, which

Her Majesty the Queen attended. I was also back on the road, gigging at nights with Gerry de Ville & The City Kings, one of the original Merseybeat groups.

In 1990, the partnership split up and Alex carried on the agency alone for the next eight years, working from home where he converted his garage into an office. In 1995, with the decline of the entertainment industry, the wheel turned full circle when he went back into the motor trade.

For some reason, God knows why, I started buying old Skodas, doing them up at home and selling them on. They were basic cars but very reliable and would run forever. However, when trade boomed and I had ten cars in the driveway, neighbours objected and that was the end of that enterprise. I also designed and built a novelty clown car, which is still being used in promotions up and down the country.

I've spent the last eleven years massively extending my property in Crossens and doing research for a book I'm currently writing on the 1950-70 Southport music scene. Although I'm 66 now, I still own a drum kit and may take up the sticks again one day before it's too late.

I don't think Buddy Rich has anything to fear.

ARTHUR PEDLAR

Arthur Pedlar was born in Southport on Sept 21st 1932 at Oxford Road Nursing Home. His family have owned Broadbents department store since the turn of the 20th century but Arthur is world famous in his own right as Vercoe the Clown. Now semi-retired, he lives in Ainsdale with his wife, Val, who recently became a local magistrate.

I had never met Arthur Pedlar until I interviewed him at his Ainsdale home in January 2006. However, I had seen his act. It was at one of the monthly luncheon meetings of the Good Turns Society, hosted by their president, Ken Dodd, and held at the Police Club in Prescot Road, Liverpool. Arthur did a five-minute spot on his unicycle and got a standing ovation.

After he had proudly told me of his performances with celebrated circuses and nightclubs in Italy, France and Russia, he showed me his collection of miniature ships in bottles. Arthur is in the Guinness Book of Records for constructing the world's smallest ship in a bottle, a hobby that paid for his unicycles.

I finally managed to get him on to the subject of his family's involvement in Southport retail trade.

It was my grandfather, Arthur Mercy, who started it all. He was an orphan who had travelled from Birmingham for a job interview at Southport Hospital Management Board. He didn't get the job but a Mr. Broadbent, who owned a single-fronted men's drapers shop in Chapel Street, offered him a post as secretary. Unfortunately, Mr Broadbent over-extended himself by opening branches in other Lancashire towns and ultimately fled to South Africa leaving huge debts. The shareholders, led by two spinster ladies called the Misses Steel, offered my grandfather the chance to run the business for them. He did so, not only repaying the debt but over a period of time acquiring neighbouring shops until Broadbents became the size it is today. It is currently part of the British Home Stores chain.

He and my grandmother moved from their house in Fir Street to 115 Roe Lane which had an empty plot beside it on which stood a rookery and bluebell garden adjacent to the old St. Cuthberts Rectory. The wood and rectory have since been developed for private housing as Bamber Gardens.

Grandfather was an Independent on the Town Council and a J.P. He and his cronies Alderman Charlie Aveling (who started the Flower Show), P.D. Boothroyd, Sam Brighouse (the solicitor), Alderman Charlton, the stockbroker, and others used to chew over the town's affairs in Thom's Teahouse on Lord Street then trot across to the Town Hall to rubber-stamp their decisions.

My grandparents had two daughters. Margaret, my mother, married Vyvian Pedlar, son of a Cornish Congregational Minster whilst Kathleen married Reuben Hainsworth, son of a Yorkshire woollen mill owner. Reuben went into the family business but my father, Vyvian, looked set for a career in show business. He entertained the troops in the Great War and performed at country house parties and actually he landed the part of juvenile lead in Daly's Musical Comedy Company on their Number One tour for five years..

However, after five years with Daly's, he returned to Southport to make his own way in retail. He and his sister, Evelyn, found premises on the first floor of 401 Lord Street with a stand on the pavement. They called the shop Wayfarers and started off by selling hand-made crafts although they soon added quality products like George Jensen silver and Lalique glass.

Vyvian still hankered after the stage, however, so he joined the Southport Dramatic Club where he met Margaret whom he married in 1929. They had two sons, Arthur (1932) and Anthony (1933) and a daughter, Angela (1938).

We lived at 78 Trafalgar Road. My father kept 3tropical fish tanks in an underground greenhouse in the garden. He was an authority on tropical fish and made more money from breeding and selling them than he did from the shop. New supplies would be brought over from Hamburg by ship to London and carried on the footplate of the train to keep them warm. My father would collect them on his bicycle from Hillside Station. This was before he acquired my grandfather's Armstrong Siddely motor car that did 64mph flat out.

In the early Thirties, Wayfarers moved premises to a shop above Connards in Lord Street. In 1935, The Leyland Arcade was purchased by Cambridge University. Most of the shops were shut and the University were anxious to restore things to their former glory. A big attraction was a tropical aquarium that father designed for the centre of the arcade. They offered Vyvian and Evelyn empty units at £25 a week each. They took four. Fred and Harry Orr, who owned Cave's Chemists in Neville Street, moved into the corner shop.

Originally, it was intended that the arcade would run from Lord Street right up to the Promenade with a tunnel under West Street. However, the owner, a Mr. Plummer, was unable to purchase the property that lay between West Street and the Promenade so he had to terminate the arcade and build steps up to exit in West Street.

The arcade had a gallery at the Promenade end where a band used to perform. Jimmy Esplin played sax and violinist Arthur Jacobson and his Orchestra were resident there.

Montague Burton, the nationwide tailors chain, bought the arcade in the early war years and changed its name to The Burton Arcade. They sold it in 1976 to the Clerical & Medical Association who granted a head lease to the company of which Broadbents was the major shareholder. It was then the name was changed again to Wayfarers Arcade.

Arthur was sent to school at Winterdyne in Waterloo Road and then to Leighton Park, a Quaker public school in Reading. He left in 1949 and joined his father and aunt at Wayfarers.

The defining moment in my life was when I was taken to Bertram Mills Circus on a site in Preston New Road when I was six. I was fascinated by the clowns and wanted to be one. I was given greasepaints for my 11th birthday and made my first public appearance at school in 1948, taking off Emmett Kelly the famous hobo clown.

Charles Lancaster, who had a workshop in Castle Street, made me my first unicycle from bicycle parts in 1948 and I graduated to a 5ft model made by Percy Manning who had a wrought ironworks in Stamford Road. Later, in 1951, I moved up to an 8ft model made by F.H. Grubb Ltd.

After I'd finished my two years National Service in the R.A.S.C., I joined Spider Austin's Troupe at the Cirque Medrano in Paris for their nine-month long 1953-4 season. I was offered a contract to go tenting round France but I made the same decision that my father had made and came, instead, into the family business. Vercoe The Clown became my hobby.

Jim Davies and his wife had run the Farmhouse Café in the Arcade for years but she died and Jim sold it to us. The place had become neglected. There were 26 girls working there on a cash-in-hand basis. We discovered that mice used to sit on the iron central heating pipes watching them cook the meals. We quickly cleaned the place up and ran it for a year with my wife's help.

We tried opening in the evening as a high-class restaurant, The Penny Farthing but it didn't take off. As the Lord Street entrance to the arcade was shut at 6pm, customers had to use the West Street entrance but that meant there was no passing trade. In the end, we rented it out to two Spanish lads who had it for a while but then Brian Kernaham moved into the premises with his bookshop and we turned the staff room and offices into furniture showrooms for Wayfarers.

Arthur's brother, Anthony, after training at Schofields in Leeds and D.H. Evans in London, went into Broadbents in the 1950's, first as a manager then on the board. Southport's other family owned department store was

Boothroyds on Lord Street. When the Boothroyd Brothers retired in the 1970's, Broadbents bought the business and the property.

The building was in a bad state, half of it had to be gutted. The pillars holding the veranda up had rotted from the inside because, when the Lord Street pavement was raised, the water outlets were blocked. The cost of repair was prohibitive as it was, of course, a Lord Street listed building.

At one time, ninety nine per cent of businesses in the street were family businesses but when pension funds and insurance companies bought up the freeholds, they were less inclined to spend money on the fabric of the buildings but Tony was not to be defeated. He brought in British Heritage and they, the council, the landlords and the tenants of all the shops agreed to pay 25% each. Without a doubt, this saved Lord Street's verandas.

Anthony Pedlar also founded Southport Film Guild and was chairman of the YMCA when it moved to Hoghton Street. Sadly, he died at the age of 49 in 1982 from complications arising from the rheumatoid arthritis he had had since his twenties. Vyvian and Margaret had died in 1979 which left Anthony's widow, Mary, in charge at Broadbents and Boothroyds after buying out the Hainsworths' shares.

BHS made an offer for the lease of the Chapel Street store in 19?? and Nigel Beale, who had been a friend of Tony's, made an offer to add Boothroyds to his chain, Beales of Bournemouth, in 19??.

The family kept the freeholds of the shops and formed a company called Lord Street Properties, having acquired the freehold in 1992.

By 1997, the rents and service charges had become too prohibitive for Wayfarers to continue trading.

The rents had to be decided by surveyors working on a 'going rate'. Wayfarers had a long and narrow floor space. Upstairs we had out workshops for framing pictures and mirrors. We needed five tills for maximising sales and for security. Five tills meant five employees earning so much a year. Our profit margins were small as we bought in small quantities yet our selling costs were high. I decided to retire and celebrate my 65th birthday by having a magnificent closing down sale.

And Arthur Pedlar did retire but his alter ego, Vercoe The Clown still performs today at venues all over the world and is very involved with international clown organisations. He is the Honorary President of the Israel Circus School.

On the day I interviewed him he was about to leave for engagements in Monte Carlo and Israel. He told me he is currently expanding the musical side of his act ready for the day when he can no longer mount an 8ft unicycle!

ALAN PINCH

Alan Pinch was editor of the Southport Visiter for twelve years. He was born in the town on January 11th 1929 and has spent most of his working life as a journalist.

Alan and his wife, Pamela live in one of the original North Meols 16th century cottages, close to St. Cuthbert's Church. When it was built, the sea came up to the back door and there were sand dunes at the front. In later centuries, there was a public washhouse behind the cottage.

My visit in February 2006 was to talk to Alan about his life in 20th century Southport.

I lived in Salisbury Street as a child and went to Norwood Road school and on to KGV. I always wanted to be a journalist. Our next door neighbour was a friend of Major Stephenson who ran the Southport Visiter at the time and my mother badgered him to get me an interview. The major told me they had no vacancies for a reporter but I could have a job on the counter taking in adverts. I thought it was better than nothing, a way of getting in, so I accepted but I was hopeless at the job. The money in the drawer never added up to what the adverts cost and the treasurer strongly advised me to seek employments elsewhere. Thus ended my brief (and first) career at the Visiter

In 1945, there were lots of jobs available. So many men had not come back from the War. I got fixed up at International Marine Radio who had established offices and a workshop by the roundabout in Leicester Street where the Chinese Restaurant is today. I was a trainee radio mechanic. They had me painting the cabinets of radio sets that were used in the liners. I stuck it for eighteen months till 1947 when I was called up for National Service. I joined the RAF who sent me on a signals operator course at Cranwell. It was the perfect thing for me as they taught me touch-typing. Couldn't have wished for a better training for a future career in journalism

When I was demobbed in 1949, I joined the Visiter's politically rival paper, the Southport Guardian. The Guardian was Liberal as opposed to the Tory Visiter. Maurice Codd was the editor and he took me on as a cub reporter. In those days, there was no official training for reporters. Just on the job experience.

When Charlie Glee, the Sports Editor, emigrated to Australia in 1950, I took over his job. I was very much involved on the production side. In 1955, I was tipped off a contact in the Liverpool Echo that the Evening Express, the rival newspaper, was looking for a chief sub-editor at their Victoria Street office in Liverpool.. I went along and got offered the job along with Sports Editor in the bargain.

In 1958, the Daily Post and Echo took over the Evening Express and Alan switched across Victoria Street to appointed Chief Sub-Editor at the Daily Post

On Saturdays and Sundays, I was covering football matches including Liverpool and Everton in the era of Bill Shankley and Harry Catterick. I often used to work a 12-hour shift from 3pm to 3am. I spent a lot of time in the canteen at 2am in the morning. My weight shot up to twenty stone due to those fry-ups.

Sports reporting can lead to some interesting experiences. In 1965, the Daily Post and Echo decided to send me to Tokyo to cover a title fight between Liverpool's boxing champion, Alan Rudkin, and the Japanese world champion, Fighting Harada. I flew from Manchester via Amsterdam and the North Pole refueling at Alaska both ways. Although he was knocked down in the first round, Rudkin got up to complete the 15 rounds but lost on points. Several members of the British press who were with me that day subsequently lost their lives in the Manchester United air crash at Munich in 1956.

In 1973, the wheel turned full circle when Alan was offered the post of Editor on the Southport Visiter.

It seemed to be a poisoned chalice. No less than three editors had died in the last three years. I thought they were perhaps trying to get rid of me. But I took the job on and found myself in charge of the Visiter nearly thirty years after they sacked me.

Alan was editor of the Southport Visiter for twelve years until he retired in 1985.

I carried on as a freelance writing the Arts Page. When I was Editor, there was a thriving arts scene in Southport. Alan Daiches was in charge of the Arts Centre and they put a lot of good shows on with food and drink served in the bar upstairs. Whether it was subsequently a good idea for the council to build and rent out another bar downstairs, creating competition and attracting a different kind of clientele, is a moot point.

Alan was always involved with sport, playing badminton, cricket and tennis.

I played cricket at the Red Triangle off Bispham Road and for the YMCA. I was in the Trinity team at the Rookery when we won the local league's First

Division title. I am also a founder member of Southport Melodic Jazz Club, which stages monthly concerts at the Royal Clifton Hotel.

As Publicity Manager for the West End Players, the last surviving church drama group in Southport, I call round at Alan's three times a year with photos and details of our latest productions for him to put in the Visiter. That's the good thing about being a journalist. You can keep going to the end.

SOUTHPORT 2006 – Photos by Ron Ellis

Pier Train

Continental Market on Lord Street

Le Petit Train passing Victoria baths & Maritime Court where the Victoria Hotel once stood

Silcock's Carousel outside Funland at the Pier Head

Funland on Pier Head near Marine Drive Bridge in background, 2006

Wesley St - one of the town's last surviving streets of small family businesses but hit by the pedestrisation of Chapel St, and new traffic routes

PROMENADE & MARINE LAKE – Photos by Ron Ellis

Ocean Plaza, Premier Inn & Brewsters Restaurant

Ocean Plaza, Vue Cinema & Restaurants

John James' plans for the redevelopment of the North Side of the Lake. But they never materalised
Photo courtesy of John James

The new Marine Drive Bridge

The Lakeside Bar, Promenade

Retail Park on site of Peter Pans Pool. Hardly a seaside attraction but it brings in the business rates!

NEW APARTMENTS – Photos by Ron Ellis

Above: 'The Academy' - luxury apartments replace The Drill Hall. Regent Court in the background

Below: The Royal Park development in Waterloo Road. Dwarfing the splendid Victorian houses around it

TOLETS – Photos by Ron Ellis

Above: The original underground lavatories in Eastbank Street Square, now turned into The Core Wine Bar

Below: ...and replaced with these 'Tardis' huts across the road outside the new 5-star hotel (about to be built on the site of the Old Palace Cinema)

Moss Lane, Churchtown from the air

Moss Lane, Churchtown looking towards Martin Mere

The Rylands' Cottage, Moss Lane (now replaced by housing development)

Dave & Jean Rylands on their farm in 1970's

Dave Rylands attends to his pigs

Edward Crowhurst at his pole vault lathe

Photo courtesy of Ron Ellis

SOUTPORT WRITERS CIRCLE

Founder Joan Nicholson, 1970's

1980's at Birkdale Library

PEOPLE & PLACES

Fancy Dress evening at the Somewhere Else Club in Neville St (where the Coliseum Cinema once stood and later the Dandy Club. In 2006 it is an amusement arcade.

Photo courtesy of Steve Dickson

Gatsby's Night Club at Prince of Wales Hotel, 1975

Photo courtesy of Ron Ellis

AERIAL VIEWS – Photos by Ron Ellis

Above: Looking east past Holy Trinity Church from roof of Regent Court, Lord St

Below: Looking across town from roof of Regent Court, Lord St

INDOOR MARKET – Photos by Ron Ellis

Above:The Indoor Market King St/Market St currently owned by Sefton Council and rented out to stallholders

Below: Interior of the market

MEOLS HALL

Above: Garden Party, 1974

Below: Spring Country Fair, 2005

Photo by Ron Ellis

Photo by Ron Ellis

PEDESTRIANISATION OF CHAPEL ST 2006 – Photos by Ron Ellis

Above: New store Primark replaces Littlewoods

Below: Building work keeps crowds away

RONNIE MALPAS – Photos courtesy of Ronnie Malpas

Serving coffee at the Mocambo 1959

Carving at his famous Palace Hotel buffet

Above: Uncle Merlin - children's entertainer and magician

Below: Ronnie at his Hot Dog Stand

'Ronnie Gage'

Uncle Merlin & his Amazing Budgie Circus

CHARLES PRESTON

Charles Preston was born at the Victoria Nursing Home and Nurses Institute, 20 Park Road, Southport on June 2nd 1936. His father was a solicitor's managing clerk with local firm, Cook and Talbot, and would have liked his son to follow him into Law but Charles preferred a career in estate agency and auctioneering.

In the early 1970's, several local estate agents used to hold regular auction sales where members of the public would bid alongside dealers like Jaggers, Mrs Nimmo from Homestead in Formby, Peter Molloy, etc and property owners, such as Frank Clarke, Eddie O'Brien, Paul Bruford and myself, for items of furniture, works of art and household appliances ranging in price from five shillings to hundreds of pounds.

By far the most entertaining of the auctioneers was a small cheery man who took the rostrum at Ellis & Sons. His name was Charles Preston and with his acerbic wit and sharp put-downs he could have made a fortune in stand-up comedy.

When I was five, I went to Winterdyne School in Waterloo Road which comprised about two or three large houses which were eventually demolished to build the Old Ben Retirement Home, itself recently replaced by 'luxury apartments'.

Winterdyne was a boys-only prep school with a uniform of grey blazers and red caps. The headmaster was George Everard who owned a large field behind the property, running along the back of houses in Oxford Road, which was used as a playing field –Cricket in summer and Association Football in winter.

Mr. Everard kept a horse in the field, which the boys were sometimes allowed to ride. He also kept rabbits in cages, hens in a large pen and goats. He would enquire how many boys would care for rabbit pie for lunch and then go out that evening and wring a few necks. Occasionally, we were given goats' milk and chicken too.

Although it was a primary school, Latin and French were taught and pupils who stayed on longer were invited to learn Greek.

Charles did not stay long enough for the Greek lessons, his parents choosing to send him away to Rydal School in Colwyn Bay where he ran The Antiquarian Society. In March 1955, he joined Ellis & Sons as an Apprentice Auctioneer, Valuer and Estate Agent.

Ellis & Sons was founded by builder William Ellis at the end of the 19th century when he set up shop at 419 Lord Street to sell the houses he had built. He later took over the estate agency of Bentinck, Saul & Co., further down the road, to form the present day business. In 1913, they acquired a saleroom at 2 Hulme Street.

At that time there were very few cars in Southport, Mr. R.V. Mather from Birkdale Lodge (at the corner of Lord Street West and Aughton Road), who had a wine and spirits business, owned one of the first. However, by the Thirties, it was a common sight to see chauffeurs waiting outside Ellis's premises beside their Rolls Royces whilst business was being conducted inside.

At one time, the company had branches in London, Manchester, Liverpool and St. Annes.

My parents paid a £210 premium for me to be taken on. My wage was £1 a week for the first year going up to thirty shillings a week for the following two years. I was articled to Aubrey Hilltout and the senior partners were Tom Bunting and Reg Jackson.

Charles left in 1967 to go to Toronto as an auctioneer for Wavil Price of College Street but returned two years later to assist in the running of the auction gallery at Ellis's along with Reg Jackson and Tom Bunting. The porter at the time was Bill O'Connor, a ell-known figure in the saleroom.

We sold some of the most expensive houses in the area. Halsall House in Halsall was one of the dearest, being offered for what was the astounding figure of £10,000 in 1955. Briars Hall, Lathom fetched £7,500 and you could get most houses in Shoreside Birkdale, including The Round House, for £5,000-£5,500.

The most unusual sale I remember in Southport was a poultry slaughterhouse in Kew where Moy Park later stood. We sold the plant and machinery. In those days, the waste products from the dead birds, the beaks, claws, bowel contents, etc., was ground up and fed back to the hens, making them unsuspecting cannibals. It wouldn't be allowed today.

There was a lot of competition in the town. David Ross and Jim Rowlandson ran Ball & Percival's auctions, Hatch & Fielding had Arthur & Gordon Fielding and John Duffy whilst Mr. Mallinson and Andrew Coburn were at Ratcliffes. T.B. Jones was still going strong in Ainsdale.

We would expect to get through 150 lots before lunch and about the same again in the afternoon. We kept household items and items that you might term the junk end of the market outside in the yard and the valuable stuff as near as possible sorted into categories so anyone coming in to buy, say, china, wouldn't have to hang around all day.

Nowadays, car boot sales have affected auctions, especially at the lower end of the market. Furthermore, thanks to television programmes, the man in the street is much better informed about antiques and fine art.

Charles parted company with Ellis & Sons in 1972 to take up a similar post in Bournemouth but that didn't work out and he returned to Southport in 1974 by which time he'd been elected a Fellow of the Royal Institution of Chartered Surveyors.

I went to work as a surveyor with the new Merseyside County Council covering Sefton and St.Helens. When the MCC was wound up, I became part of Merseyside Residual Body dealing with the disposal of surplus properties. I ended up with the new Merseyside Development Corporation mostly dealing with compulsory purchase matters, and also acted as a part-time surveyor to the Trustees of the Liverpool Empire Theatre.

I retired in the late 1990's but in my spare time, I'm a volunteer steward for the National Trust at Rufford Old Hall.

I have been an active member of Southport Dramatic Club since 1966, and a past Chairman. In 1972-3, I was chairman of the Little Theatre Guild of Great Britain.

When I did this interview with Charles in his Churchtown home where he lives with his wife, Barbara, (they have two children and a grandson), I was impressed with his meticulously indexed collection of local memorabilia including a complete collection of S.D.C. programmes since the company's inception.

ALAN PROLE

Alan Prole was born in Crosby on April 6th 1928. He lived on the Wirral in his early years, moving to Southport in his early twenties. For over two decades, he reported on Southport FC's matches in his role as Sports Editor for the Southport Visiter. He is married to Sylvia and they live in Churchtown. They have four children and six grandsons

As football reporter for the Southport Champion, I regularly sit alongside Alan in the Press Box at Haig Avenue, suffering the fumes from his interminable pipe.

My father was sports editor on the Liverpool Echo, writing under the name of 'Ranger', so I suppose I followed him into the profession.

We first moved to Southport when I came out of the RAF and I got a job at Bob Martin's in Hoghton Street. They made pet foods, shampoos and other products for animals in a factory behind their offices in Hoghton Street where Stoker's furniture showroom now stands. They were market leaders in their field and one of Southport's biggest employers.

I went to Smart's College in Hoghton Street to learn Typing and Pitman's Shorthand. There was no journalistic training in those days; you picked it up as you went along.

When my father retired from the Echo, he went freelancing from an office above William Deacon's Bank in Birkdale Village and I joined him there. We wrote a lot of sports reports for local and regional papers and wrote programme notes for different clubs.

Walter Pilkington was Sports Editor of the Lancashire Evening Post based in Preston and in 1968 he asked me to join them at their Southport branch office in Tulketh Street.

The Liverpool Echo and Manchester Evening News also had offices in the town in those days and a man used to sell evening papers from a pram outside the National Westminster Bank at the corner of Neville Street and Lord Street.

A year later, I moved to the Crosby Herald and started the Walton Times but within three years, I moved to the sports desk at the Southport Visiter. In 1978, I became the Group Sports Editor until I retired in 1993.

I covered all Southport's matches during that time. I remember going to Swansea with the team one year and the coach was vandalised and we couldn't get back. An ex-Swansea player called Mel Nurse had a B & B and he put all of us up until a replacement vehicle arrived next day.

Sadly, Southport lost their league status to Wigan Athletic in 1978 and dropped down to the Northern Premier League. They might have gone out of existence were it not for the intervention of the Hall Brothers in 1981. However, the last three years have seen a revival and this season they have returned to full-time for the first time in 28 years as members of the Nationwide Conference. Also, a group of young supporters have formed the 'Trust in Yellow' Supporters Trust which bodes well for the future of the club.

Over the years, people like Charles Lambert (BBC), Paul Joyce (Sunday Express), Dave Bassett and Dave Prentice (Liverpool Echo) have all worked for me.

I was chairman of the local N.U.J. branch. We used to hold meetings at the Blundellsands Hotel and the Grapes in Freshfield.

When I retired from the Visiter, I kept on the freelance work and at 78, I still report on Southport's home matches for the Liverpool Daily Post.

When I asked Alan about his social life, I was surprised at how many activities he took part in.

I married Sylvia at Holy Trinity Church in 1956. We used to go to the weekly rep at the Scala Theatre where they had a coal fire burning in the foyer in the winter. I took dancing lessons with Madame Wheeler on Lord Street and we used to go to the Floral Hall on a Saturday night where the big bands played. There were many cinemas in the town in the fifties and I received a lot of complimentary tickets through the Visiter.

I appeared in the pantomime at St. James's youth club; I was a Sunday School teacher at Birkdale Congregational Church in Trafalgar Road, where we also put on plays, and I also played tennis, at Hillside and Weld Tennis Clubs.

In 1985, Sylvia and I joined the Southport branch of the C.H.A. (Countrywide Holiday Association), which later became the Southport Walking and Social Club. We travelled by coach on alternate Sundays to places like The Lakes, North Wales and The Peak District and members would set off on walks of varying lengths.

The early vehicles, supplied by Jones's Coaches were none too reliable and once a wheel fell off and we were stranded in the middle of nowhere for ages. I was Chairman from 1995-8 but we stopped going in 2000 due to family commitments.

As many as 350 people were members at one time and we regularly filled two coaches but numbers have dropped off in recent years as people, especially young people, join other things. And there are three other walking clubs in Southport, the Southport Ramblers, the Southport Fell Walkers and the U3A Walking Club.

We are also Folk Dancing enthusiasts. We used to meet at Hatherlow Hall in Leyland Road but since that was demolished to make flats, we meet at St. Peter's Church in Birkdale.

For many years, we've ben members of Southport Gramophone Society that used to meet at St. Mark's Church (The 'Jam Chapel'), at the corner of Derby Road and Sussex Road, but that is now a doctor's surgery so we meet at the United Reform Church in Trafalgar Road (ex. Birkdale Congregational). We used to have forty to fifty members in the seventies but it's half that now. Each week we listen to classical music, chosen by a different member or a visiting guest who gives a short talk about the selection of records.

My main sporting interest is Crown Green Bowls. It's a very popular sport in the town but, again, fewer young people are taking it up. There's Southport Parks League, a Southport L.V. League and a Southport Veterans League.

I'm a member of the Hesketh Arms club. We have a bowling green between the pub and Botanic Gardens but I don't know for how much longer. We get little support from the brewery and so many pubs are being turned by the big chains into family restaurants. Many greens have been lost in recent years like the Park in Birkdale, the Imperial and the Shakespeare. They become car parks or are sold for housing,

Then there is the constant trouble with vandals. Bedford Park in particular has suffered prolonged damage to its greens and premises and little seems able to be done to stop it in today's liberal climate.

On Boxing Day, Alan nearly died when he fell down the steps of the grandstand at Haig Avenue and fractured his skull. Happily, he has made a remarkable recovery and I'm looking forward to sitting with him in the press box this season. Especially as he's given up smoking!

PHIL RODWELL

Southport born Phil Rodwell runs southport.gb.com, the town's premier unofficial website, where he posts under the soubriquet of 'On The Spot'.

I knew Phil back in the 70's when he repaired the roof of one of my properties in Victoria Street, in the days before he became the Voice of Southport in cyberspace. Now, in 2006, we had lunch in the lounge of the Royal Clifton Hotel and he explained how it all came about.

I was born on Dec 1st 1959 at the Christiana Hartley Maternity Home. The family lived in Victory Avenue and my mum still lives there. I went to St. Simon's school in High Park, then Norwood Road and finally Meols Cop.I left school at 15 and got a job as an apprentice mechanic at Brockfield and Buntings who had a Peugeot and DAF dealership in Ainsdale but I only lasted six months. I was a bit of a tearaway as a teenager.

For the next few years, I did various general labouring jobs until I became a self-employed roofer in 1978 in partnership with my older brother, Paul. We got a lot of work round town including fixing the copper roof on the old Baptist Tabernacle by the roundabout at the top of Scarisbrick New Road. Paul still runs that business today and I help him out occasionally on roof jobs.

I got into buying and selling property and renovating old houses, turning them into flats to rent out. I still have these.

So when did the dramatic change from jobbing builder to media mogul and computer whizz-kid take place?

I'm not a computer whizz-kid, I leave that to my partner who does the technical work on the website. No, it all started when I tried to buy domain names. My idea was to buy names that people might want and sell them on. I tried to buy radio.com but, after agreeing to sell to me, the company who owned it accepted a better offer. As compensation, they offered me any ten domain names for nothing. I picked ten with Southport in the title including southport.gb.com.

My original idea was to use it as an online local directory and sell advertising but I soon realised if I wanted people to look at it, I'd have to provide news content. The web-page was set up by Steve Ashcroft who came in as my partner to handle that side of things. My job was to bring in the news stories and sell the advertising.

I soon found out I had one big advantage over the two local newspapers, the Visiter and the Champion, in that I could get the latest news online immediately. The Visiter only came out on Wednesdays and Fridays and the Champion just on a Wednesday therefore, if something happened in the town on a Thursday night it couldn't be reported in the paper until the following Wednesday by which time it was old news. I'd had it on the site for six days.

Sometimes I get aggro when people don't want photos taken but news is in the public interest. The Visiter aren't happy with me, although they've used a couple of my photos, without my acknowledgement I might add. But I get on all right with the Champion and they've happily used my photos from time to time.

Surely it couldn't be that easy. Newspapers have a staff of full-time trained reporters following up stories. I asked Phil how one man on his own could compete with them?

Easy. I've built up a network of people to provide me with stories as they happen. Taxi drivers who are driving around the town all day will ring or text me whenever they see something happening. I have many contacts throughout the town!

I could vouch for that. When I got stuck in a lift at Regent Court last year, one of the residents phoned the fire brigade. Two fully manned engines turned up within minutes (the fire station is just across the road!) but Phil was there before either of them.

I usually get between 10 and 15 calls a day and they are all voluntary helpers. The only paid employee is my full-time salesman who is on the road selling advertising space and he works on commission.

People who have forthcoming events to advertise like shows and plays just e-mail us in with the details. We give results of local sport and have sections for public announcements plus links to local organisations such as churches, drama groups, schools, sports teams etc. as well as a photographic section on Southport Past that is very popular.

I've photographed Noel Gallagher, Paul McCartney, Ken Dodd and other celebrities and sold pictures to the nationals.

The big thing about southport.gb.com is that it's interactive and the newspapers can't compete with that. People can post their opinions instantly about every news item that goes on the site and other readers join in and open up a dialogue. That can't happen with newspapers where replies to readers' letters are spread over weeks. I'm not responsible for what people say although, of course, libellous and obscene things are deleted.

Nobody said a life in the paparazzi was easy. At the last General Election, police ejected Phil from the Floral Hall after Sefton supreme Graham Heywood had him ejected.

He said Sefton Council did not recognise the N.U.J as media, and he said that anyone could get a card, and I wasn't allowed to take photographs. The police confiscated my camera but they gave it back to me later. Sefton Council have refused to send southport.gb.com their press releases for the past five years.

There could be a dilemma for them here then because Phil is contesting Norwood Ward for the Conservatives in the May 2006 local elections. How did he come to stand for the council?

George Halsall and David Woodfire suggested I'd make a good candidate as I feel very strongly about certain issues in the town. I asked for Norwood ward because High Park and Blowick is where I belong. It's a big task. The Lib-Dems have held the seat for the past 25 years but I feel I have a chance as I can relate to people in the area. I get people who say I use the website for electioneering, which I suppose I do, but then I also publish the posts by people knocking me and accusing me of this. People are entitled to their views.

A fortnight after this interview, the local elections were held and, sadly for David Cameron's party, Phil failed to defeat David Sumner who has held the seat for the Lib Dems since 1998. However, I have no doubt he will be putting up at the next election and, with his highly visible public profile as the mouthpiece of southportgb.com, he must be in with a shout.

JOHN ROSTRON

John Rostron was born in Derby in 1945 but he comes from an old Southport family. He studied Dentistry at Liverpool University and, upon graduating in 1970, joined the practice at 22 Hoghton Street that he still works in today.

He has also served a total of 67 years as a school governor at Farnborough Road, Greenbank High School and King George V College and is a member of Royal Birkdale Golf Club, Southport Rugby Club and the Old Georgians.

In 2006, John was awarded an M.B.E. for services to Higher Education. He is married to Christine. They have four children.

I usually see John's face bearing down on me as I lie back apprehensively in his dentist's chair. He has tended to my teeth for most of his working life. However, in 2005, he sat me in a less intimidating chair at his home in Hillside and gave me a potted history of the family.

My grandfather was Septimus Rostron who went to Toronto Canada in 1899 to seek his fortune as a builder. With his wife and five children, he returned to Southport from Toronto in 1926 just before the slump and set up a joinery and building business. Whilst in Canada he was the bandmaster with the Canadian army through the trenches of the 1st World war and led the Canadian army into Mons after the 11th hour of the 11th Day in 1918. Of course Southport is now twinned with Mons.

His company built numerous houses in the town, in Waterloo Road, Hastings Road, Clovelly Drive, Ryder Crescent, Dunster Road, Guildford Road and Heathfield Road. His developments in St Clair Drive and Silverthorne Drive in Churchtown commemorate his time in Canada, St Clair being named after the St Clair River in Toronto and Silverthorne after the street where members of the family lived in Toronto. Silverthorne Drive was built on the Croxton School playing fields that backed onto the old Preston-Southport railway line.

The business was wound up in 1980.

My father, Ken, attended the very first day of King George V School in Scarisbrick New Road in 1926 on his return from Canada. He was bilingual, fluent in French and English. He went on to study medicine at Liverpool University following initially, a surgical career gaining his Fellowship in Surgery from Edinburgh.

He moved into General Practice in Church Street joining the practice with Ron Caile, it subsequently became Caile, Rostron and Graham. He was doctor to many local companies such as Holland Toffee in Virginia Street and was the first factory doctor at Mullards in Crossens. He looked after Hesketh Park

Hospital, New Hall isolation hospital and Sunnyside Hospital. He would do upward of 30 house calls in a day.

My first school at 3 years was Farnborough Road Infants where they had canvas beds and we had to have an hour's sleep every afternoon in the first year.

Miss Davison was Head of Infants and Arthur Loveridge Head of the Juniors.

I joined 55th Trafalgar Road Cubs attached to the United Reform Church in Trafalgar Road.

In 1956 I passed the 11+ and moved to KGV School. Joining Evan's House as my father had been a member, and my brother Peter was already there. I joined the Railway Club, the Scientific Society and the Jazz Club.

In the 1950's I also remember going down to Chapel Street Congregational Church to see the slot car racing at the Southport Model Club, the first slot car racing in the world, they also had a great model railway which fed my enthusiasm for railway modelling.

With this propensity for belonging, I suggested that John should have taken up joinery as he seemed to join every club he could find. He agreed that he could easily have followed his grandfather into joinery but he found dentistry as his calling.

After KGV, I did a year at Southport College under Mr. Hollis then went up to Liverpool University Dental School for 4 years and a term. Today the course takes 6 years with the vocational training year. At University I was President of the Dental Students Society bringing the Student Rugby sevens and the Conference to Liverpool for the first time.

After qualification I joined the old Wilkinson-Robb practice that started in 1884 and was the oldest practice in the North. When I joined on 1st January 1970 the partners were Roberts, Bell and Duce. I had two patients on my first day and by Easter I was fully booked. Payment was on piecework paid by the Government two to four months in arrears after completion of the treatment. I became a partner in July 1971.

I remembered my own horrifying childhood experiences as a patient under a Mr Hilton in Queens Road (known locally as The Butcher) in the days when dentists put a rubber mask over your face and forced you to keep inhaling this evil-smelling gas until you finally lost consciousness. In some cases permanently, as I pointed out to John.

Which is why that has all finished. From 1970-1990 we did 20-30 anaesthetic cases in a morning where patients were put to sleep and it was never a problem. But then came the Poswillo Report in 1990 that stated that all anaesthetic cases had to be administered in hospitals. There had been some high profile cases in the press of children dying under the anaesthetic in the dental surgeries. The result was that costs rocketed, and the work under anaesthetic was discouraged, a retrograde step for small children. The anaesthetic fee in practice was £11.00 this rose to approximately £150 performed in hospital in 1990.

Dentists were among the first drug addicts. They used to be very partial to giving themselves a quick whiff of nitrous oxide (the "laughing gas" anaesthetic) after a hard days work. At Hoghton Street in 1922 Bertie Davis made the mistake, after work one Friday night, of strapping the mask on his face with a piece of elastic to leave his hands free. He was found dead on Monday Morning.

In 1948 nearly every dentist did NHS work and the fees were good. Southport became a jewel in the crown of the NHS as the only strictly private practice was done by Stanley Hilton-Collinge in Lulworth Road and Eric Neubert in Queens Road.

Dentistry was revolutionised in the early 60's with the invention of the high speed air rota, which ran at 250,000 revs per minute the old slow cord driven drill ran at 25,000 revs per minute. This made drilling a lot faster and much less painful for the patient. Along with the introduction local anaesthetic for routine work, dentistry became painless.

From the 1920's to the early 1950's it was not unusual in the cities for a girl to have all her teeth removed and a set of false teeth given to her as a 21st birthday present, to save the expense of dental treatment in later years. Teeth are much healthier today thanks to improved oral hygiene, diet and fluoride in toothpastes

In the 1970's we made about ten sets of full dentures a week, mainly for older patients. Nowadays it is rare to find a full set of dentures worn by anyone under 65.

It is also becoming more difficult to find an NHS dentist in 2005. We still take NHS patients as but more and more dentists are going into the private sector and the time is approaching when we will turn away NHS patients.

John's big hobby in life is collecting music and memorabilia of the 50's and 60's and he is well known in this field. He has an impressive collection of rare singles, a jukebox and old-fashioned pinball machines. When Buddy Holly's Crickets come to the U.K., they stay at John's house and use it as a base. When American sixties star, Freddy Cannon, ('Way Down Yonder in New Orleans', etc.) played the Southport Theatre in 2004, Freddy and his lead guitarist (who happened to be Bobby Vee's son), dined at John and Christine's. In the world of rock'n'roll, you don't get much more cool than that.

I first met The Crickets when they came to the Floral Hall in 1974. The first booking they did for me was in 1999, a charity event in aid of the Southport branch of the National Osteoporosis Society of which my wife, Christine, is Chairman/Secretary. We put them up at our house and since then they've become good friends of ours. We've been to Nashville several times to stay with JI Allison and his wife, Joanie, and we've all been on holidays together.

I was also the Tour Manager for the Crickets on 3 occasions over that period, it isn't too attractive being on the road but different.

In 2001 the Crickets, JI Allison, Joe B Mauldin, Sonny Curtis along with Glen D Hardin had nothing to do on the Monday morning before sound check at the Concert, so they went down to KGV College to give a music symposium to the students.

John is also keen on sport and, as might be expected, he soon joined the appropriate local clubs.

Whilst at KGV I played Cricket for Southport & Birkdale Juniors, being the junior secretary, and at the age of 18, I joined The Royal Birkdale Golf Club.

I played Rugby in the First XV for 3 years at KGV School and gained my colours, enabling me to wear the special blazer, this along with 1/2 colours at Cricket. I also Played and Captained the Southport Rugby Club Colts, before moving into the First XV, playing between 1961 to 1971 and gaining my colours in the first year playing at full back.

There were no leagues but we organised fixtures with other clubs such as Waterloo, Orrell, Preston Grasshoppers, Vale of Lune and Bury. The wing forward for Bury was John Whittaker who, as the Chairman of Peel Holdings, now owns The Trafford Centre, John Lennon Airport and Manchester Ship Canal.

I was lucky enough to play with a number of future internationals including Tony Neary at University and Frank Anderson at Southport, and of course Harry Foster the well known local historian, who was in his twilight years and recognised as the best uncapped second row in the Country.

In 1971-72 we raised money to rebuild a major part of the clubhouse just before the Centenary of the club, Southport RUFC being one of the oldest in the Country.

When I was organising the entertainment through the 60's we had a function on two out if three Saturday nights. It could have been an up and coming Merseybeat group from Liverpool but on the balmy summer nights I used to book George Bailey's Tropical Seven Steel Band. George came over from Barbados in the late 50's, and I'm delighted to say that he, his wife Lynn and the family are still patients of mine today.

When at KGV I booked the Beatles to play at the Prefects' Dance at Christmas. The fee was £10-10-0d (£10.50p.), but there was a proviso that if they had a hit record in the meantime they could be released from the contract. As we know, they had a hit in October 1962 with 'Love Me Do'. Brian Epstein pulled them out so we replaced them with local favourites Rhythm & Blues Incorporated for £5-5-0d. (£5.25p.).

I joined The Royal Birkdale Golf Club in 1962, the annual Junior subscription being two guineas. Today it is over £1000. I went round in 62 with a 14 handicap when I was 22.

I was the personal roving steward for Peter Thompson's winning last round in the 1965 Open. At the 17th par 5, he hit a 3 wood off the tee and a 3 wood from the fairway to within a couple of feet and got an eagle 3. He hadn't spoken to me before that shot but came over and said 'you don't need a driver round here, just be accurate.'

The top professionals shared the clubhouse with members and Arnold Palmer, Jack Nicklaus and Lee Trevino, amongst many others, would sit down have a chat and a drink with them after their rounds.

John has also been very involved in education in the town for the last 23 years, serving on four boards as a school governor.

The hardest work was after the 1986 Education Act when, within certain parameters, schools had control of school budget spending,. I took 4 schools through that transition.

I first joined Farnborough Road Board in 1983 and was on it for 14 years serving for 13 years as Vice-Chairman to Iris Sell who was a superb Chairman of Committees. Ironically, our best achievement there was in 1984 when we won our fight to keep the remedial class to support slow learners. This would not be acceptable today but then it made front page of the Southport Visiter.

I joined Greenbank High School Board in 1987 and was appointed Vice Chairman at the first meeting, serving as Vice Chairman for 6 years and then Chairman from 1992 to 2002. In the first year we moved to Local Management of Schools and I attended 52 meetings at the school in that year.

When the Royal and Ancient came to Royal Birkdale in 1983 they paid Sefton £10,000 for the use of the playing fields and school for corporate hospitality and to erect the tented village. Yet the school itself did not benefit from the disruption.

After the Education Act of 1986, the Governors became responsible for that agreement so, in 1990, I negotiated a fee in excess of £125,000 for the exclusive use of the fields and buildings. This was index-linked for the Open in

1998. With a grant from the Sports Council, we built the floodlit All Weather Pitch that has been available to the school and community ever since.

I became a Governor of KGV College in 1987 and became Chairman of the Board a year later, a post I still hold today. I spend 3 or 4 evenings at the school and I have the best Board in the Country, acknowledged by OFSTED. We have a cross section of people with a gender split of 50/50 and an age profile from 18 to 65+. It really does keep the mind active.

John lives in the house in Ryder Crescent once owned by Monty Bloom who, as L.S.Lowry's first big patron in the late 60's, at one time kept 90 Lowry paintings in the building. John has lifted the floorboards and searched the loft but, regrettably, has not found any left behind.

When I went along in February 2006 to take his photo for this article, John had just been appointed Captain of Royal Birkdale Golf Club. Sadly, I was a day too late for the champagne.

JOE RUANE

Joe Ruane was born in County Mayo, Ireland in 1924 into a family of farmers. He came to Southport in 1949 when he was working as an agent for the Co-operative Insurance Society. In 1958, he rented the top two floors of the Kingsway building and opened the Marine Club. In 1964, he moved to premises in Coronation Street and stayed there until 1988 when he retired.

When I was a DJ in the seventies, I played for Joe Ruane on the top floor of his Marine Club in Coronation Walk from 10.30pm to 2am every Wednesday night. On the first floor they had cabaret, upstairs was the disco. They got a very mixed crowd in there ranging from teenagers to pensioners. It was never 'posh' like Toad Hall and occasionally there were fights. I owned several flats by then and many of my tenants were regulars at the club. They would come across to the disco and hand over their rent along with a record request.

But the building hadn't always been a club, in the fifties it had housed Madame Tussaud's Waxworks, and Joe Ruane wasn't your run of the mill club owner.

My first business in Southport was a grocer's shop at the corner of Old Park Lane and Newton Street, which I ran with my wife, Eileen, whom I'd married three years previously. I also worked for eight years as an agent for the Co-op Insurance. After visiting Russell's Club in Manchester, which offered bingo, dancing and a restaurant, I decided I wanted to run my own club.

In 1960, I approached Mrs. Ormerod who owned the Kingsway Café on the Promenade, to see if she would rent me part of the building. Mrs Ormerod's mother had built the Kingsway in the early part of the century and had operated it as a very successful café. She served fish & chips with bread and butter and a cup of tea to coach loads of day-trippers on three floors of dining rooms. The kitchens were in the basement. She was known as Rabbit Lucy as she skinned and sold rabbits from a stall on the Promenade.

During the Second World War, the Civil Service had occupied the top two floors of the building during the War but they were now empty. Mrs. Ormerod leased them to me for £450 a year.

We had 1000 members within a few weeks. Bill Melvin and Frank Maloney from the Co-op helped me. I made the first floor into a social club. You didn't need a licence in those days, you just had to register the premises as a club and have 25 members, with a chairman, secretary and a resident committee. We hired a three-piece band, Dave Collins was the compére and we put in a roulette table. George Greenhalgh played piano. At the time, there was only the Floodlight Club, Dorothy's Barn Club, The Scheherazade and the Glenpark Club in town. The pubs closed at 10pm and there were no buses after 10.40pm. The road sweepers were out at eleven and the streets were deserted.

Twelve months later, we opened up the second floor and called it the Marine Club. We charged two shillings to go in and started having acts on a Tuesday night, most of them from the Mike Hughes Agency in Liverpool. We tried everything from wrestling to bingo and cabaret Ronnie Appleby started the Monday nights with beat groups. He called it the Jive Club. Many of the Merseybeat groups like Gerry and The Pacemakers and Mark Peters and The Silhouettes played here. On one night in July 1962 when Ronnie arranged for The Beatles to appear, we charged three shillings and sixpence admission on the door and I paid the group £8. I've still got the flyer for that dance today. It's been valued at £1,000.

In 1964, Mrs. Ormerod sold the Kingsway to John James and Joe had to find alternative premises.

I found a place in Coronation Walk. The ground floor was a car showroom when I took it over but before that it had been Madame Tussaud's Waxworks with a life-size model of a man with a swinging blade in the window representing the Spanish Inquisition. I ran the car business for a time with a partner, trading as C & R Motors. I did the upstairs up myself and opened up as the Marine Club. It was an instant success. I'd kept a list of all my old members and when we opened on that first night, they were queuing right round the corner on to the Promenade.

On the ground floor, the cars weren't doing so well so I tried opening up as a carpet shop instead but it wasn't much better and, in the end, I made the showroom part of the club. Joyce McDowell was my cashier and Eileen acted as the hostess, running the club with me. We never had problems with drugs in all the time I had the club. I put on gambling there for a while but it was mainly a cabaret club with, later, a disco upstairs.

The Marine was always a sociable club. A lot of the clientele became personal friends of Joe and Eileen and they held many charity events at the club, especially for the Knights of St. Columbo. For a time, Joe was financial secretary of that organisation, which met regularly at St. Marie's Church. In one year they raised £17.000 for charity.

The Marine Club later changed its name to Champers but when Eileen died in 1994, Joe lost a lot of his enthusiasm. In 1998, he sold the club and retired. Currently it is a wine bar called The Republik.

DAVE RYLANDS

Dave Rylands was born in July 1929 in Didsbury. His father was branch manager of Edmond Walker, bearings specialists in Manchester. The family moved to Southport in 1934. He and Jean have three children, nine grandchildren, two great-grandchildren and recently celebrated their golden wedding.

When I first knew them in 1973, Dave & Jean lived in a Victorian farm cottage in Moss Lane, Churchtown with their three children. The house was always full of friends and neighbours popping in for a friendly chat and a cup of tea. I was one of those neighbours as I lived in a cottage further down Moss Lane, beyond the Three Pools opposite where the old Isolation Hospital once stood. I went out for a quite a while with their daughter, Cath, who later married Conservative Councillor Mildred Monk's son, Geoff, a meteorologist.

In 2006, sitting beside a coal fire in the cosy lounge of their new bungalow overlooking the Old Links golf course, Dave explained to me how they came to live in Moss Lane.

When I first arrived in Southport, we lived in Liverpool Avenue in Ainsdale. I went to school at Merchant Taylors' in Crosby and then on to Hutton Agricultural College. I met Jean at St. John's Youth Club in Ainsdale in 1947. Jean lived in Woodvale Sidings in what would have been an old railwayman's cottage, alongside the old Cheshire Lines railway route and where Moor Lane is now. Down the track was a crane and weighbridge.

During the War, as teenagers, we used to put out nightlines on Ainsdale and Birkdale beaches to catch fish, such as cod, plaice, whiting and skate. We'd go shooting rabbits and game in the sand hills.

In 1948, I worked on Boundary Farm, a dairy farm on Birkdale Moss. I was there two years then moved to Anderson's Farm in Nixon's Lane. The farm is still there but now you have to cross Heathfield Road, which wasn't built then, and go down Philip Drive. The Ministry of Defence used to keep aircraft parts on wasteland down Nixon's Lane and Jean used to eat her sandwiches there at lunchtime.

We got married in 1953 and our first home was a caravan with a smallholding alongside in Southport Road near the Crematorium. We rented the smallholding for £1 a week. The caravan was £3 a week. We had an acre of growing ground and I kept a few hens and pigs. Several people in Southport kept pigs until well after the war. There were half a dozen piggeries in Guildford Road alone.

We grew salads and potatoes on the land. 1953 was a slump year. I used to take the produce on my motorcycle and sidecar up to the market in Cazneau Street, Liverpool. Later I bought a 1936 Austin Ascot pick-up.

In 1955, we moved to Moss Lane when I got a job on Shaw's Farm and the tied cottage came with the job. I kept a few pigs at the back. Sir Vivian Naylor Leyland owned the farm but Jeremy Simpson ran it. Only ten years after the War, It was still very countrified round the back of Churchtown and Crossens. When Jeremy retired, I got the tenancy of the house and outbuildings and a one and a half acre field. I bought more pigs and grew cabbage and potatoes but the ground was too wet so I ended up turning the pigs out.

From 1961-1966 I worked for Harold White on his arable farm on Martin Mere and built up the pig herd at home. I had farrowing pens, weaner pens and sow stalls and the effluent went into a sewer, which the council protested was overloaded. Moss Lane was never sewered until 1961 and then not all the way to the end where they had septic tanks.

The pig herd was expanding to such an extent that Dave built a piggery. He also started to breed chickens and built a broiler house. This side of the business flourished too and, two years later, he doubled the size of the broiler house.

We kept 10,000 chickens in that broiler house and we had 40 breeding sows. I also kept two or three calves as well.

In 1972, prices for chickens hit a new low. I used to supply Southport Broiler Services, which was run by John Craig, who had the Bold Hotel on Lord Street, and Bill Clough. They also had Moy Park at Kew. They had a contract rearing scheme whereby they supplied the newly hatched chickens and feed and we shared the sales. It was an eleven-week cycle. Eight weeks from day-olds to killing the fattened birds, then three weeks cleaning out the sheds. There were about twenty growers in the group including Bill Taylor at Woodend, Bill Abram at Banks and Bill Walker in Bankfield Lane.

As late as the 1960's, Moss Lane still retained a lot of its rural and agricultural heritage but that was soon to change.

Moss Lodge was up the road from us but it was demolished in the late Sixties and a row of bungalows put in its place. Fine Jane's Way was built on Prescott's Farm in the Seventies. Scarisbrick Estates, who owned the land, wanted to build houses on the Old Links Golf Course right up to Victory Avenue and re-site the clubhouse to Pitt's House Farm. Their idea was to move the golf course to the other side of Three Pools on Robert Hesketh's land but in the end, the deal never happened and the Golf Club secured their future by buying the land themselves.

In 1989, the Ryland's cottage fell under the demolition hammer.

Scarisbrick Estates sold the land for building and, along with Bridge Farm, the whole plot became Foster's Close. Because we were a tied cottage, they had to rehouse us so they built us this bungalow in Pitt's House Lane.

The pigs and chickens might have gone but Dave still soldiers on, helping his son Ian who is a ground works contractor providing digging services for builders.

DAVID HARRISON – All photos courtesy of David Harrison except 'Natterjack, by Ron Ellis

1950's The Plaza Cinema, Ainsdale

1960's The Moulin Rouge (Ballroom Dancing)

1970's Tiffany's (A Mecca Dance Hall of Disco)

2006 The Natterjack (A Toby Inn pub/restaurant)

Ronnie Bateman and his Orchestra at The Moulin Rouge

David Harrison judges 'Miss Hot Pants' at Tiffany's

GINGER McCAIN

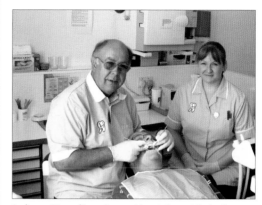

JOHN ROSTRON

Ginger at Bank House 2006
Photo courtesy of Ron Ellis

John attending to patient Ian Nicholson watched by dental nurse Katie Ashworth in his Hoghton St surgery
Photo courtesy of Ron Ellis

Ginger, Ken Dodd & Jonjo O'Neil congratulate Red Rum on his Grand National Victory at his Upper Aughton Rd Stable
Photo courtesy of Ron Ellis

Buddy Holly's Crickets give a music lesson at KGV College Joe B Mauldin, Glen D Hardin, Sonny Curtis and J.I. Allison

Flowers & Birthday Cake for Red Rum's 21st. He devoured the oatmeal cakes in seconds!
Photo courtesy of Ron Ellis

John with The Crickets at Royal Birkdale Golf Club, JBM, SC, John & JIA
Photo courtesy of John Rostron

JOE RUANE – Photos courtesy of Joe Ruane

Marine Club, 1970's

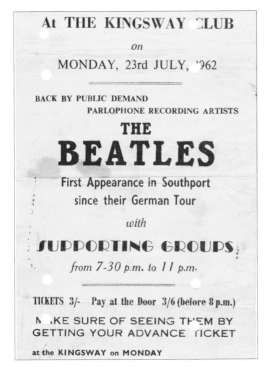

Poster for Beatles Show, 1962 (valued at £1,000 in 2004)

Joe's wife, Eileen, with U.S. rock 'n' roll legend, Gene Vincent

Champers, 1990's

Republik, 2006

Joe Ruane, George Greenalgh, guest and Raymond Taylor at the Marine Club, Raymond Taylor played the organ in the Municipal Gardens for many years.

RALPH GREGSON

Ralph launching the Sefton Lottery with Ken Dodd & Jean Jessop in the Floral Hall Gardens

Photo courtesy of Ralph Gregson

Ralph on the last boat to leave the Pier - the Lytham Lifeboat, 1986

Photo courtesy of Ralph Gregson

Ralph attached by wrestling star Giant Haystacks in the Floral Hall Gardens, 1982

Photo courtesy of Ralph Gregson

JEAN ALEXANDER

Jean (3rd from left back row) at a Civic Dinner

Jean judges the Southport Rosebud Competition

Jean on stage in a S.R.C. production

TOMMY MANN

Tommy driving his father's minature train at New Brighton, aged 15

Photo courtesy of Tommy Mann

Marine Lake from Pier Head, 1991

Photo by Ron Ellis

PETER MOLLOY

Molloy's first removal van

St James Street Shop

Molloy's shop corner of Lord St and Seabank Road

PETER EATON

Bessie Eaton, founder of June The Florist Shops, aims 'Best in Show' Prize at Southport Flower Show

June's flagship shop corner of Lord St and Eastborne St

June's shop in Birkdale village

PAT BALL

The Shelbourne Hotel

Photo courtesy of Pat Ball

The bar at the Shelbourne Hotel. Note the advert for the long-established Bothy Folk Song Club

Photo courtesy of Pat Ball

Valentino's Restaurant, Lord St

Photo courtesy of Pat Ball

MARTIN CONNARD

Connards Jewellers on Lord St, 1889

Connards in 2006

Martin at his pigeon loft

ROY ADAMS – Photos courtesy of Roy Adams

The Kingsway Club, Promenade

Liverpool doormen, Ray Adams in 2nd from left. At far right is Tommy Barton who owns The Sands in Ainsdale

Roy beneath the famous elephant's head at Shorrock's Hill, Formby

La Corniche Restaurant in the Kingsway

Roy in his body building days

Roy 2005 at home with Charlie

Photo courtesy of Ron Ellis

Botanic Gardens

Prince Edward takes his seat along with Mayor Norman Jones

Botanic Gardens Lake

Albert (Hangman) Pierrepoint in Botanic Gardens

Gordon Herod driving the Botanic Gardens Train

BARRY WOMERSLEY

R&B Inc by the plane that flew them from 'Ready Steady Go' in London to Woodvale Airport for their Floral Hall show.

Photo courtesy of Barry Womersley

R&B Inc at Lord Astor's resdence, Cliveden. LtoR: John McCaffrey, Alan Menzies, Mike McKay, Barry Womersley, Pete Kelly

Photo courtesy of Barry Womersley

Inner Sleeve. LtoR: Ian McGhee, John Surguy, Barry Womersley, John McCaffrey

Photo courtesy of Barry Womersley

Jasmin T. LtoR: John McCaffrey, John Surguy, Barry Womersley, Alan Menzies, Alan Solomons

Photo courtesy of Barry Womersley

Barry with Inner Sleeve at Royal Clifton Hotel, 2004

Photo courtesy of Ron Ellis

Apoco Music Wesley St, 2006

Photo courtesy of Ron Ellis

TREVOR HITCHEN – Photos courtesy of Ron Ellis

Stanley Matthews shakes hands with Trevor at Trevor's benefit match at Haig Avenue. The referee is Arthur Ellis. 1954

Trevor's newsagents stall in the Ribble Bus Station

Trevor judges the English Rose competion with SFC captain, Tommy Kinloch, and SFC manager Lem Newcomb who owned a newsagents shop in Seabank Road

Outside Trevor's first newsagents shop in Coronation Walk. Next door is Madame Tussard's Waxworks, later The Marine Club

'Smithies' newsagents in Hoghton Street

RON ELLIS

E.&M. Sherlock - Grocers & Confectioners at 25 Forest Rd, 1921-1957. Pictures is Ron's Mother - Isobel Sherlock (Note the verandahs)

Photo courtesy of Ron Ellis

Southbank Road Tennis Club, cica 1930 (Isobel Sherlock front right)

15 St Lukes Grove

Photo courtesy of Ron Ellis

95 Manchester Road

Photo courtesy of Ron Ellis

52 Promenade between Queens Coaches and the Queens Hotel

Photo courtesy of Ron Ellis

D.J-ing at West Lancs Yacht Club, 1970's

Photo courtesy of Susan Hiley

MIKE SWIFT

Mike Swift was born in Paradise Lane, Freshfield on June 4th 1953 and moved to Southport in 1969. He is best known in the town as the one-time Chef Executive of the Chamber of Commerce.

I had never met Mike before my interview with him in December 2005 but his name was familiar to me through the local press as he was constantly in the news due to his position on the Chamber of Commerce. However, as he explained to me, his early career was very much determined by his mother and stepfather.

My mother's second husband is Ken Smart whose father, Aubrey, was the manager of Waring and Gillows who had taken over what was originally Pursers furniture emporium in Lord Street. My mother worked in the shop that was next door to Booths supermarket. Ken was the Removals Manager. W. & G. was owned at that time by Manny Cousins, one-time chairman of Leeds United FC. Manny decided to close the Removals Dept. so he offered it to Ken to run as his own business. It was a very fair deal as Manny included the vehicles, the staff and the shop's delivery contracts as well as the operation of two warehouses in Aughton Road and Manchester Road. The business was named Drury Smart.

Mike did not immediately go into the removals business full-time, preferring to qualify in an industry outside the family business.

I did my City & Guilds in Radio & TV Engineering at Riversdale College in Liverpool and joined Visionhire on Chapel Street as an apprentice service engineer in 1970 during the boom in colour TV, ending up as the Service Manager in Ormskirk

In 1974, Mike took over as Manager at Drury Smarts. Prior to 1974, no professional qualifications were required in the management of the transport industry but he completed a six-year course leading to an International Certificate of Professional Competence that included operating commercial vehicles for hire and reward, estimating volume of goods to be packed, packing methods and materials, choice of suitable vehicles, sea and air freight routes, customs procedures and appointment of agents overseas, etc.

At the time, there was a lot of competition in Southport and a lot of characters too. There was John Moss operating out of Bath Street North, John McDowall (Isle of Wight Farm in Stamford Road), Doyles (Southbank Road), Molloys (St. James Street), Pickfords (Southbank Road), Bev Gregory (Ainsdale), Joe Grimley (Sussex Road), Poulsons (Sussex Road), Howards (Bispham Road), Campbells (Ainsdale) and Walter Carters in Virginia St who were part of the Harrods empire.

Every morning, the drivers all used to meet up for breakfast at Andy's Café turning Kingsway into a 'who's who' of pantechnicons. Very few drivers changed firms and owners would not poach staff, preferring to recruit and train up their own people.

At the time, the numbers of vehicles any removal company was allowed to own was strictly limited and regulated by the Ministry of Transport so the only way to expand the business was to buy out other local firms.

We bought Howard's and Walter Carter the latter also bringing to us a huge warehouse in Virginia St, a building that was originally Southport's first hospital. We later acquired and operated John Moss's outfit. John had at that time one of the best removal men in town, Alan Beggs, who also worked part time as a doorman in the Southport clubs. Alan's uncle Roden had been on the road with Waring & Gillow at the creation of Drury Smart and was a tremendous support to my stepfather in the early Drury Smart days.

We had some good contracts, including the annual Southport Flower Show other exhibitions and some interesting commercial jobs too. We emptied the Kingsway when the Karani family, who also owned the Grand Casino in Lord Street and the Charlie Chester Club in Soho, sold to Roy Adams. In the Kingsway they had a fabulous wine cellar and specially imported Italian furniture. The high rollers would eat off gold plates. We put new 'flying safes' into the Grand by crane through the first floor 'Disney' windows in the very early hours of a Sunday morning. We also took the old ones out, negotiated a road closure with the council and popped the new air conditioning system on to the roof.

Many family homes have relocated with Drury Smart's assistance, both here and overseas. When international football star Graham Souness left Liverpool for a new family home in Spain's Balearics, I arranged and supervised the complete job, flying out the family's many pets and the delicate home contents, including the transportation and installation of a brand new, brilliant white grand piano, over long road journeys and a couple of ferry sailings.

In 1993, Mike was ready for a new challenge and he sold Drury Smarts to their biggest competitor, Pickfords, although he continued in the business for a time, managing first their Preston/Southport/Blackpool group then their Lancaster/Isle of Man operations.

In 1994 he was appointed the first full time Chief Executive Officer of Sefton Chamber of Commerce, a non-political body representing local businessmen that was formed from the old Southport Chamber of Trade in 1992. Back in the 1980's, had been their youngest chairman of Southport Chamber, following his election from the membership of Drury Smart.

At its height, we had over a thousand members and some clout. We combined with South Sefton, which was mainly industrial and manufacturing, and Mid-Sefton, which included the neighbourhood retail area around Formby. Southport, of course, had a strong reputation for its tourism, unique individual retailers, the professional services sectors plus the multiples.

My predecessor, Jim Robson, coped with pay and display which had just been brought in and divided businesses, residents and councillors alike. A lot of businesses were against it and there was the longest protest march in the town since the Marshside shrimpers. The council wanted it because they knew it would bring them in a net million pounds a year so why should they worry about who got upset over what was just another tax?

In 1994, at the back end of John Major's reign as Prime Minister, Sefton was awarded for Southport challenge funding of £7.2 million, with EU money added, as part of Government Single Region Regeneration Budget.

The public money was used to stimulate business in the town through economic regeneration. We brought in inward investment. Apollo Leisure, for example, took over at the Theatre and the Floral Hall, the biggest leisure facility on Merseyside. We also embarked on a campaign to improve the housing stock in the town, some of which was seriously dilapidated.

At first Central Government could not believe that Southport also had serious social problems so near to the magnificent Lord Street with, for example, sub-standard housing. However, we took them with partners round some multi-occupation houses in the town centre in streets like Alexander Road and Scarisbrick Street where, at worst, there were open lavatories on the landings shared by families living on different floors. One property even caught fire during an inspection visit and at one site a family were discovered living in a Portacabin in the rear yard. We had to act quickly in making grant aid forthcoming to support tenants via their landlords.

The Central Southport Partnership, comprising members of Sefton Chamber of Commerce, Sefton Council, Voluntary Groups and residents, has been responsible for the building of many creative regeneration projects stimulating business, creating jobs, supporting residents and recreation including the new swimming baths, the improved lighting in Lord Street by using unique white street scene halogen lamps and the early refurbishment of Hesketh Park.

The local authority had not got the cash to fund several heritage projects that badly needed work so we identified in partnership key strategic areas and then sourced the right agencies for funding. Eventually, we got £2.7 million together, for the Pier from the Heritage Lottery; E.U.Objective One, Sefton Council and the developers of Ocean Plaza as part of the planning arrangements when the land was available to be released.

Mike also became secretary of Southport Pier Trust, responsible for the complete restoration of the town's pier.

In 1860, Southport was the first town in Britain to build a leisure pier. Ours is the second longest pier in the country, after Southend, and we are the first to restore such a long pier.

I resigned from the Chamber in 1992, after eight years service, to start Inglemell Ltd., my own expert witness practice and specialist business consultancy.

However, I'm still involved in public life with Queenscourt Hospice and I recently completed a charity marathon eight-hour commentary session to an audience of over 1000 gathered on the banks of Southport's Marine Lake at the inaugural Southport Dragon Boat Race.

In May 2006, Mike stood as a Conservative candidate in Meols Ward in May 2006 against the popular Lib-Dem incumbent, Councillor David Rimmer, but failed to win the seat.

Mike travels regularly across America with his wife, Sheila, and has written a book about U.S. contemporary country music. When I read the manuscript, I knew immediately that Mike's true calling in life was to be a country music disc jockey and in July 2006, he rang me to say he had landed a job on the newly formed Southport Community Radio station.

I've got my own twice-weekly show called 'On The Road Again', recalling my sojourns in America and featuring contemporary Country Music.

What did I say? Next stop Nashville?

KLAUS 'TIM' TIMMERMAN

Tim Timmerman came over from Holland in 1962 as an apprentice baker, serving his time at Mellors confectioners in Lord Street. He went on to own the company and has since gone on to become one of Southport's most successful businessmen, being also the current owner of the Royal Clifton Hotel on the Promenade.

When Tim bought the Royal Clifton, I had already been disc-jockeying there for many years, which was when our paths first crossed. And I continued to play there for many years afterwards, the New Years Eve parties being particularly enjoyable gigs.

Now, in 2006, here I was, back at the hotel, listening to Tim's inspiring story starting with why he set out to become a baker.

I was born on September 1st 1943 in Langedy, a village near Amsterdam. When I was eight, I was rescued from drowning by the local baker. My mother sent me to his bakery with a bunch of flowers. He gave me a cake and I thought what a nice warm place it was to work in and you could eat as much cake as you like.

At 14, I worked as an apprentice baker and attended a part-time Confectioners Course for two years at a Technical College in Amsterdam. When I gained my National Diploma as a Master Baker at 19, I came to England on a student exchange scheme between my college and the Colquitt Street Catering College in Liverpool who sent me to Mellors for six months as a trainee. It was the time of Merseybeat and The Beatles and I loved it.

Mellors in Lord Street was the oldest trading company in Southport having been established in 1840 as Dean Confectionery. Amelia Mellor, neé Ashworth, was an apprentice who returned in 1872 to buy the business from the Dean family. She and her husband, Gilbert Mellor, who also owned the Scarisbrick Arms Hotel, renamed it Mellors. Their daughter took over in 1904 helped by her own husband, James Hall, who developed new lines producing jam and groceries and later went on to found the Spar grocery group as well as run a successful local wholesalers. The shop remained in the Mellors family until 1977.

On my first day I arrived at the Ribble Bus Station and was met by two of Mellors' apprentices and drank pints of ale, something we never got in Holland where it was all lager. I found lodgings with a Mrs. Dix in Bath Street North and while I was here I met my wife, Shirley, when she came with some friends into the El Cabala coffee bar in Eastbank Street as I was drinking a coffee there. I saw her and thought she looked interesting.

Shirley Hepton was a dancing teacher at Betti Bersi's Dance Academy in Coronation Walk and became one of the founders of the Southport Dance Academy in Mornington Road. Tim must have made an impression because when he went back to Holland to do his National Service in the Dutch Navy, after a six-month stint as a pastry chef in a Jersey Hotel, Shirley took a job with Shell in Amsterdam. They married in 1965 when Tim was demobbed and he joined Rank Hovis McDougal as bakery foreman in Manchester and then Bradford.

In 1971, I got a tip-off from my boss that there was a café for sale in Southport that would suit me. It was Long's Café on Lord Street and the owner, Mrs. Pettitt, was retiring because she couldn't cope with the change to the new decimal currency. I bought the café, named it The Dutch Chef and converted the upstairs kitchen into a bakery. I had a staff of just five.

In 1974, I took over Hughes' butchers shop in Chapel Street, next to the corner of London Street, and turned that into the second Dutch Chef. When the whole block was rebuilt, and River Island took over that pitch, I transferred the business to London Street. To cope with the extra demand, I bought Rimmer's betting shop in Stanley Street, behind my first shop, and converted it into a bigger bakery. It has since become The Oast House.

Stanley Street boasted a nice little community at the time. Bert Sharples ran an entertainment agency and restaurant there. This was called the Mardi Gras and on most days the cast from the Scala would meet for lunch and a gossip. The famous cartoonist, Bill Tidy, had his office opposite and was at the height of his fame with The Cloggies strip. We got him to do a cartoon of our staff. Just up the road was The Elbow Room, one of those afternoon, members-only, drinking clubs which continued serving to members after the pubs were shut..

When Philip Hall, grandson of Amelia Mellor, decided to retire in 1977, he offered me the chance to buy Mellors and I was delighted to do so. The business consisted of the Lord Street shop and a bakery in Hulme Street with a total staff of twenty. There was also the old Madge Brewers shop and café in Botanic Road, opposite St. Cuthbert's Church, but that was bought by Claude Verité, who was the manager there at the time, and it became Claude's Patisserie.

I went on to open more Mellors shops and by 1990 they were in Ainsdale, Formby, Churchtown, Birkdale, Ormskirk, Skelmersdale, Liverpool and Maghull.

They all had cafes. And I changed the name of my Chapel Street shop to Mellors leaving just my first shop as The Dutch Chef.

I was having problems with my neighbours in Hulme Street about the noise from the bakery so I bought the building in West Street that used to be Broadbents' old funeral parlour and the bakery that belonged to Booths Supermarket when they were on Lord Street. This later became the Warehouse Restaurant and the current chef in charge of the bakery is Claude Verité. How things go in circles.

But trade was increasing beyond the capacity of these premises so Tim bought land and buildings behind the old Blowick Hotel (now the Thatch and Thistle) in Crowland Street belonging to Mullards factory dating back to 1953 and moved his bakery there, building houses and flats on the Hulme Street site.

I only wanted 6,000 square feet but I got 16,000. Mullards made radio valves there and 90% of the workforce were women and I inherited 17 ladies toilets and one gents for the manager, so I had to split them in two.

I couldn't expand the retail trade fast enough to make use of all that space so I bought Forshaw's Bakery in Tarleton, purely for the business. Supermarkets with their in-house bakeries were eating into the trade of small businesses. The customer profile was changing. We were selling more lunchtime snacks than cakes. I started to supply supermarkets and multiples like ASDA and the Co-op. With over 200 stores on their books, Mellors essentially became manufacturers rather than retailers.

By 1996, we had moved into contract catering with my son, Mark, running Mellors Catering Services. Many companies were concentrating on their core business and contracting out things like cleaning and catering. We now run canteens and staff restaurants in over 68 establishments in the North West including Matalan, Deurrs Jam, Securicor, Southport College, Stanley School and KGV College.

In 2004, Mellors sold the Crowland Street premises and relocated to a custom built factory on the Slaidburn Industrial Estate in Crossens. A link remains, however, at the Blowick site as one of the streets in the Servite Houses housing association development there is named Mellors Close.

So, alongside all this expansion in his bakery business, how did Tim find the time to fit in buying the town's biggest hotel?

I used to attend the weekly Rotary Club lunch held there every Wednesday and was asked by the President to speak to the management about the quality of the lunches. It was then that I was told that the owners, the Prince of Wales Group who owned a total of eight hotels, wanted to offload the Royal Clifton.

The fabric of the hotel was in a poor state and the interior badly needed upgrading, lacking many of the basic facilities like en-suite bathrooms that are de rigueur in all hotels in this day and age.

However, the price was right and I bought it in 1986 in partnership with Bob and Paula Yoxall, who are now retired. We built a health and leisure club with a gym, swimming pool and sauna, which is open to private members as well as residents, and we joined the international Best Western Hotels marketing organisation, which ensures all members maintain a certain standard. Five years later, we bought the Balcony Inn Hotel on the M58 in Skelmersdale and renamed it the Lancashire Manor but we sold that in 2000.

We are one of the largest employers in the town with 350 in the catering division and 100 at the Royal Clifton.

Tim's involvement in business life led him into joining various organisations, the obvious one, perhaps, being the Southport Marketing and Enterprise Bureau.

As a hotelier, I realised the importance of attracting businesses and people into the town, which in the Eighties was stagnating somewhat. Both the Chamber of Commerce and the council seemed to be losing their focus. As soon as we formed the bureau, things started to happen and Sefton Council appointed two marketing officers and has since grown into the successful 'Tourism Department, based on the corner of Portland Street and King Street that used to belong to Dewars, the local beer and spirits wholesalers.'

Coming from a horticultural family himself, it was natural for Tim to align himself with the 'Save the Southport Flower Show' movement when Sefton Council shamefully abandoned the historic event in 1986.

We set up the Southport Flower Show Company and persuaded local businessmen to guarantee £3,000 each to stage the 1987 show. We put the emphasis back on the horticulture element, attracted 30,000 visitors and made a £6,000 profit compared with the council's £60,000 loss the year before. Since then, visitor numbers have increased from 30,000 people to over 100,000.

I became the Marketing Director and, in 1994, the council handed over the control of Victoria Park to the company, granting us a 60-year lease in return for an annual bouquet of flowers. Importantly, it allows us to use the 34-acre site for other events.

Like so many people in this book, Tim shows little sign of slowing down as all his businesses continue to flourish, although retirement is beckoning on the horizon. Yet, oddly, I got the impression he'd be quite happy to don his white coat for the day and spend a few hours in his bakery making the vanilla slices and gingerbreads for which Mellors is famous.

SHEILA WALSH

Sheila Walsh was born Sheila O'Nions in Birmingham in 1928. They moved to Southport during the War and she met her husband, Des, at Holy Family. For many years they ran the family jewellers shop in Chapel Street. Sheila is Life President of Southport Writers Circle and a member of Southport Soroptomists . She has written over 30 historical novels and is a Vice President of the Romantic Novelists Association.

I first met Sheila when I joined Southport Writers Circle of which she was a founder member. She had just had her first novel, 'Golden Songbird' accepted which spurred on the rest of the group to get writing. Indeed, had it not been for those weekly meetings, in which everyone was expected to produce a piece to read out on the night, I might not have become a published writer myself. Instead, each week I wrote another episode of 'Journal of a Coffin Dodger' and my literary career was launched. The Writers Circle has a lot to answer for.

At her Churchtown home, Sheila related to me how she came to live in Southport.

The family moved from Birmingham during the War to avoid the bombs. I went to Notre Dame School in Birkdale and I met my husband, Des, at Holy Family. We married in 1950 at Holy Family Church.

We used to put on plays in the old Holy Family School House in Mornington Road. Phil Furnival built the sets and Des did the electrics. There was a piano on the stage and we had dances with home made bands and records. I went on to join the Southport Operatic Society.

For many years we ran the family jewellers shop at 39 Chapel Street. Des's father, who came from Oldham, started the business in 1926. There were no national chains in those days and not as many jewellers' shops as there are today. We knew all our clients. Later, someone bought the whole corner and rents went up. Eventually they knocked the whole block down. We moved round the corner to London Street. Des was not originally a jeweller. He had actually trained in electrical goods at Turner and Booths on Lord Street.

I remembered Turner and Booths myself. Every year on Cup Final day, they allowed the public into their showrooms in Stanley Street to watch the match on a range of televisions that they probably hoped to sell to them after the game. We didn't have a television at home in the fifties and my mother and I were regular attendees at Turner and Booths Cup Finals for many years.

Our daughter, Fran, married Andrew Gregson of Ball and Gregson's the bakers and confectioners in Churchtown, so we ended up with two well-known local businesses in the family.

The London Street shop closed in 1987. We sold the lease to a young couple who opened up as a clothes shop but it didn't last. The multiples could sell goods cheaper than the small shopkeeper could buy them.

I joined Southport Writers Circle in 1971. It started out at the Technical College as a Creative Writing class run by Joan Nicholson who was a successful romantic novelist from Yorkshire.

There were afternoon and evening classes but they were merged in 1973. At 9pm, when the lesson finished, most of us would go back to Joan's house in Sussex Road. During the holidays, we decided to carry on meeting every Thursday evening at each other's homes.

The first Southport Writers Seminar was held in October 1974 at the Scarisbrick Hotel. The speakers were crime novelist Jack Wainwright and local actress Thelma Falls-Hand. The Seminar ran every year for over thirty years.

Sheila's first book, 'Golden Songbird', was accepted in 1973 and published the following year by Hurst and Blackett. It won the Romantic Novelists Association Netta Muskett for New Writers. 'A Highly Respectable Marriage' won the 1984 Elizabeth Goudge Award. Sheila served as Chairman of the R.N.A. from 1985-87 and is now a Vice President.

In 1975, the Technical College banned smoking in the classrooms and, as many of our members smoked, we found new premises in rooms above a fruit warehouse in Market Street, also used as rehearsal rooms by The Garrick Players. We stayed there until the end of the seventies when we moved to our present home at Birkdale Library.

When Joan Nicholson died in 1980, Sheila took over as Chairman of the circle and was elected Life President in 1986.

Every week, our members would read out a piece they had written during the week and the others would then criticise it, favourably or otherwise. Several of our members went on to become successful published authors. Lyn Andrews was working at Marks and Spencer when she joined the circle, now she is one of the country's top saga writers. Ron Ellis has had over a dozen crime novels published and Marie Murray has written 32 Mills and Boons books that have been translated into over two dozen different languages. Mills and Boon have also published over 20 books by Roger Sanderson (suitably disguised as Jill Sanderson). Kate Conlon was already famous for her TV adaptations when she joined us and is still writing today. Other members who have had books published include Eve Gavin (as Jessica March), Alma Nyman (as Alma Ashley), Alison Chisholm, Mary Johnson (Angela Noel) and Alan Joyce.

Sheila and Des are now retired and, sadly, not in the best of health.

SIR RON WATSON

Ron Watson was born on May 24th 1945 at South Shields of an English father and Canadian mother. His family moved to Formby when he was thirteen and he came to Southport in 1966 when he married Lesley Barber, daughter of Alderman Harold Barber and granddaughter of Sir Herbert Barber.

Ron Watson is a great pop music fan, his interests encompassing classic rock'n'roll, jazz and blues. He contributes articles and record reviews to various magazines, which is how I know him best. We have had telephone discussions over the years about Merseybeat and the merits of certain blues singers but the first time we actually met was when I called at his Birkdale home in February 2006 and he told me about his career in tourism and politics.

After leaving Waterloo Grammar School, I joined the passenger department of Canadian Pacific situated in the Royal Liver Buildings in Liverpool but I left in 1968 to join Morrisons Travel Agents Ltd. in the Cambridge Arcade.

It was the advent of the package tour holiday and people were flocking to Spain and Italy instead of Blackpool and Brighton.

The manager was Henry Laycock and we became good friends. When he later set up on his own as Laycock Travel, I joined him at his Birkdale Village office. Our biggest customer was Cooperheat run by local businessman Peter Cooper who had invented a revolutionary method of stress relief on pipework. At the time he was the town's biggest employer. We were flying 15-20 of his employees out every week, mainly to the Middle East, the Gulf States, Scandinavia and the USA.

The only mistake I made when handling this account was when they asked me to book a technician to go to Panama City which I duly did except I booked him into Panama and I found out later they were referring to Panama City in Florida.

In 1982, Ron went back to Morrisons Travel and expanded the company, opening branches in Formby and St. Helens. Eventually they also had offices in Leyland and Ormskirk.

I went in part time, three days a week, as general manager. Ormskirk had a big business account but in Southport there was huge competition from other agents.

The company was broken up in the 1990's and Ron, who had already ventured into local politics, decided to make this his career.

I was only 21 when I put up for Birkdale North ward at a by-election. I won at the second attempt in 1969 and served three years. In 1974, after the reshuffle in Sefton, I represented Birkdale South and Ainsdale and remained there until I finally lost an election in 1991. But I got back in again the following year in Dukes Ward. From 1983-91 I was leader of the Conservative Group and Leader of Sefton Council when we had a majority.

I've represented local government at national level in a number of areas. I was Deputy Chairman of the Local Government Association and the Regeneration Board, I chaired the Tourism & Environmental executives and was on the European Body for Commissioner of Regions. But there are always 20-30 local issues to be resolved for my constituents at any one time, many of them business problems as my ward covers the town centre.

Sefton's hung council has, in my view, hindered efficient local government in our area. There is little innovation and a lot of muddled thinking and the cabinet system means that about ten people effectively make all the decisions which in turn restricts the ability of back bench members to make a real difference as decisions can only be questioned after they have been made which, to me, is a funny type of democracy.

I asked Ron what he regarded as his most important achievements as a councillor.

When I was Housing chief in the early 1970's, the then Labour government declared that any unsold housing estates could be bought by local authorities and used for council housing. At that time, I was trying to develop a scheme to build 200 council houses on a Greenfield site in Marshside but I was coming up against all sorts of bureaucratic difficulties.

I decided to go to Westminster to see the Secretary of State, Peter Shore and put it to him that if councils could buy up privately built housing estates, why could they not commission them in the first place? He said he had never been asked such a question before and there was not a form to cover such a situation. However, when I pointed out that we could develop the site in half the normal time and save 25% of the cost in the bargain by commissioning the work ourselves, he could see the logic in it and gave me the go-ahead.

Broseley won the competitive tender to build the houses, the bulk of which have now been sold to ex-council tenants, and nobody driving through that estate would realise that these were council houses as they were built to private dwelling specifications

Something else I am proud of is the extension of the remit for Housing Associations that give lower paid people the ability to obtain a tenancy and was something of a halfway house between traditional council housing and the private sector.

Personally, I think the introduction of Housing Associations is a scandalous Government-inspired move to get rid of the private landlord, possibly the last bastion of the amateur businessman in today's global business world where small shopkeepers have been all but wiped out by the likes of Wal Mart and Tescos and many other businesses ruined by bureaucratic red tape, high taxes and EU regulations like the iniquitous Health and Safety Act.

However, not wishing to spend the next few hours arguing with Ron about this, I quickly moved on to his other big interest, and mine, namely music and, in particular, Merseybeat.

My Dad bought an expensive and powerful radio in the 1950's and I used to tune into the American Forces Network broadcast from Germany that played some amazing sounds. The first record my Mum and Dad bought for me was an Elvis Presley 78 of 'Hound Dog' c/w 'Don't Be Cruel'.

When I worked at Canadian Pacific, I used to go to The Cavern in my lunch hour and saw The Beatles perform there many times. I also saw them at the Kingsway, the Floral Hall, the Cambridge Hall and the Odeon. One of my best friends at school was Gibson Kemp who took over from Ringo Starr in Rory Storm and The Hurricanes and later married Astrid Kirchherr, Stuart Sutcliffe's ex-fiancé. Kingsize Taylor, who for years had the butchers shop opposite the Crown Hotel in Birkdale, made what I think is the best ever Merseybeat album, which he recorded under the name of The Shakers.

And, as I pointed out to Ron, he also made the best sausages in town.

BARRY WOMERSLEY

Barry Womersley runs Apoco Music in Wesley Street and is Southport best-known pop musician from the 1960's. A virtuoso guitarist and vocalist, he has had success in the record charts and on television and still performs regularly in the area. His wife, Connie, writes the 'Munro the Mole' children's books and they have a daughter, Katy, who is an archaeologist.

I have known Barry since he was in The Diplomats as they were one of the first groups I used to book when I was an agent. We have never lost touch since.

I was born at Christiana Hartley's Maternity Hospital, like most of my generation, on May 18th 1945 and went to school at Holy Trinity and Meols Cop.

I left school at fifteen and had a variety of jobs. I started at Hartwood Hosiery in Crossens in 1960 putting nylon stockings on hot aluminium legs. I lasted a week.

I then delivered wallpaper for Slinn's in Tulketh Street, riding rounds on a bicycle with a big carrier on the front. On my second week, I crashed the bike and they sacked me.

My next move was to Diamond Plastics in Bridge Street where I had to blow up footballs with a compressed airgun, a dangerous job. Ray Marshall, who played in The Berry Pickers, and Clive Griffiths of Timebox were there too. A trio of aspiring musicians! I was paid one and three pence an hour and left after three weeks.

Next stop was Melias in Chapel Street where I was on the cooked meats counter. A fortnight later I joined Victoria Carpets on Lord Street where I actually stayed a year as a trainee carpet salesman before moving to Garrick Engineering in Compton Road as a tea boy.

As well as these 'proper' jobs, I also did spells as a lifeguard on the beach, worked the bingo halls on Pleasureland and laboured on various building sites.

It showed how easy it was to get jobs in those days.

But Barry's real future lay in music as a singer, songwriter and lead guitarist.

I learned to play the harmonica at seven and my Dad taught me three chords on the ukulele when I was eight. I got my first guitar in 1954, a Hofner made in Germany. They were hard to get and it cost 89 guineas on hire purchase from Cranes in Liverpool.

I immediately formed a group with friends from school, Phil Nixon (rhythm), Johnny Horton (tea chest bass) and Pete Chapman on washboard. I was nine years old. We called ourselves The Hot Strings Skiffle Group and were together for about six years. We played Lonnie Donegan stuff at first but moved on to Elvis and rock'n'roll.

In 1958, we played at The Cambridge Hall on the same bill as The Quarrymen who later became The Beatles. They were about four years older than us and that is a tremendous difference at that age. Had I been born four years earlier, I'd probably have been in a Liverpool band.

In 1961, I formed The Diplomats with Kevin Finlayson (drums), Dave Tollins (bass), Quentin Hagarty (rhythm). We played at local venues like The Glenpark Club on Lord Street; Capo Nero in West Street, owned by Peter 'The Greek' Johannides and later the British Legion Club; All Souls Youth Club and the Queens Hotel when we were on with The Beatles.

Barry's big break came in 1963 when he replaced George Eccles as lead guitarist with Rhythm & Blues Incorporated.

Jim Turner of Arcade Variety in Liverpool was just taking over the band. Pete Kelly was the lead singer, John McCaffrey played bass, Mike McKay was on rhythm and Alan Menzies on drums. Alan has been playing in The Bootles for the last twenty years and now lives in Denmark.

We broke the attendance record at the Floral Hall in 1964 when we were flown into Woodvale in a five-seater plane from London where we'd been recording 'Ready Steady Go'. They put two 26" televisions onstage so the audience could see us on the show.

Our record of 'Louie Louie' got to No. 40 in the Hit Parade and we toured Scotland, played at Lord Astor's house, Cliveden, scene of the infamous Profumo scandal in 1963, and performed at numerous society do's and debutante's dances in London. When we did the London School of Economics, they gave us scarves and we were able to eat in the canteen for two shillings (10p.) for a three course dinner when we were in London. We played with The Beatles again, this time at the Kingsway.

Thom Keyes based much of his book 'All Night Stand' on R & B.Inc.

We played three years running at the Edinburgh Festival at a club called The Place, where Sean Connery's brother was on the door, and at Oxford University where we slept on the floor of the Bodleian Library.

We also backed American blues legends like Champion Jack Dupree and Memphis Slim. Pete wanted to do more blues and I preferred pop so I left in 1966 and joined Johnny Hutchinson and Ray Marshall in a new version of The Big Three which lasted a year until I formed Jasmin T.

We recorded 'Some Other Guy' as Jasmin T on the Tangerine label but it did nothing. However, we did some good gigs like The TopTen Club in Hamburg and a tour of Denmark. At home, we played the Kingsway and the Dixieland Showbar at the Pier Head.

In 1968, I went to play at a restaurant in Scarisbrick called La Tava, now Master McGraths. Their slogan was 'Wine, Dine and Dance'. I was there, on and off, for almost fifteen years.

The same year, I wrote the incidental music for Tony Tenser's film, 'Haunted House of Horrors' starring Frankie Avalon and filmed at the Palace Hotel in Birkdale. The hotel had been shut for two years but everything was still in place but covered by layers of dust. There were still coffee cups on the tables. It was like the Marie Celeste. And, the hotel was supposed to be haunted in real life, which gave it an extra edge.

Barry's greatest success was yet to come. In 1972, he formed a new band called Inner Sleeve.

We stared as a 3-piece and were resident at Maxim's in the Brunswick Hotel four nights a week. It was the most popular venue in town. We went on ITV's famous 'Opportunity Knocks' talent show hosted by Hughie Green and won three weeks running. EMI signed us and we made a record called 'Here We Go' written by myself and John Surguy.

Inner Sleeve lasted three years after which Barry played with a variety of bands in the area as well as doing solo gigs or duets with his brother, Don. He also did a substantial amount of studio session work in London including demos for singers like Cliff Richard.

I started doing more songwriting myself and in 1975, Ariola/Hansa records signed me as a solo singer. I wrote a song called Gypsy, produced by Bruce Welch of The Shadows but they released a song called 'Standing on the Corner' instead. I later sold Gypsy to Roger Whittaker who recorded it in 1976.

In 1985, I recorded Barry singing three country songs I had written which I put out on my own label (and are available on CD today from my website!!). He has a Don Williams/Jim Reeves type of voice and could have been a big country star had he been born in Alabama instead of Southport.

Don & I recorded another of Ron's songs, 'Nicola', which came out in 2003 by The Womersley Brothers on Mike Brocken's Mayfield label which specialises in Merseybeat.

Today, I am a shareholder in Apoco Music shops and I run the Wesley Stret branch. There are a lot fewer people on the street since the pedestrianisation scheme and also since Waitrose replaced Morrison's supermarket in Tulketh Street.

Barry is an expert on vintage musical instruments and known to his customers as 'The Guitar Doctor'. He also dabbles in antiques and curios from time to time and, in the 1980's, opened an antique shop in Market Street called, naturally, Gypsy.

I'm still writing songs, doing the odd session work and still gigging with different bands like Big Fish and Kingsize Taylor & The Dominoes as well as solo work round town.

I'm trying to persuade Barry to produce a CD collection of all his recordings and songs. I'm sure there is a big market for it as he has a legion of fans in the town. Getting him to find the time to do it is another matter.

JEAN WOODS

Jean Woods has worked as a nurse in Southport for 42 years. She was born in Grindleton, Yorkshire on May 6th 1944 and came to Southport in 1962.

When I had the idea for this book, I wanted to include someone who had nursed in both the old and new hospitals in the town and could see a difference in the style of nursing. Kath Lloyd, who had been a nurse at the old Southport Infirmary, but not the new one, suggested I attend the Florence Nightingale Service at Holy Trinity Church where there would be a plethora of nurses, many of them retired. And it was there that I met Jean Woods with the lovely smile and the Kevin Keegan hairdo.

A week later, I interviewed her at her Birkdale home.

I came to Southport on a visit to my sisters-in-law who took me to the Autumn Fair at St. Stephen's Church in Banks. It was opened by Amy Drinkwater who was the Matron at the Promenade Hospital. I got talking to her and she asked me if I'd considered a career in nursing. I was working in a factory at the time making clothes for Trutex. Nursing seemed a more attractive alternative, so I left home to come to Southport and started at the Promenade Hospital as a cadet nurse in the Out-Patients Dept. in January 1962.

The hospital issued us with our uniform, starched caps and aprons, and they laundered them for us. Cadet nurses wore purple dresses with green belts; SRN's wore blue dresses and belts and sisters wore navy blue dresses and belts. All nurses wore white aprons and caps and black stockings or tights with black flat shoes.

Travelling to and from work, however hot the weather, we had to wear our 'outside uniform' which consisted of a navy blue raincoat and cap with the obligatory black stockings and shoes. I once went into the Dolphin Café next to the Grand Cinema on Lord Street one afternoon in my outside uniform and, when I got to work, the theatre sister tore strips off me because someone had reported seeing me in it off duty.

Cadet nurses were responsible for cleaning as well as nursing. On a Wednesday when I had to polish brasses, clean the wood panels round the walls and wash the woodwork in the Out-Patients. Nurses were responsible for cleaning the sluice room and the lockers in their ward.

The Matron came round with her entourage every day inspecting the Wards. At the Prom, there was a Matron, Deputy Matron, Admin Sisters, Ward Sisters and two Sister Tutors. How they could do with Matrons today.

The Prom was designated a medium-sized hospital with Orthopaedic and Paraplegic Wards, an Ear, Nose and Throat Dept for adults and children, male and female medical wards and one of the top specialist Spinal Injuries Unit in the country.

We worked split shifts, 8am-1pm then back from 5-8.30pm. A day shirt ran from 8am to 5pm, a night shift was 8pm to 8.15 next morning. Sometimes, we did a 'late' which was noon till 8.30pm.

Food was prepared and cooked in the hospital kitchens, put into steamers or on to hot plates and taken round the wards on dinner trolleys. The nurses knew which patients were on special diets and made sure they got the correct meals.

At that time, there were several hospitals in the town including Hesketh Park, Sunnyside, Fleetwood Road, Hawkshead Street Children's and St. Katherine's and Christiana Hartley maternity hospitals. New Hall in Scarisbrick was originally an isolation hospital for infectious diseases, but later became a rehab unit after surgery before it was demolished and replaced by houses.

After six months as a cadet, Jean started her two-year State Enrolled Nurse training, moving round all the wards. In July 1964, on becoming an S.E.N., she moved to the Hawkshead Street Children's Hospital where she was responsible for training care assistants.

The hospital had a baby ward, boy and girl wards, an isolation ward and a special school for children with learning difficulties.

I stayed there for five years until 1969 when I joined the staff of Bradstock Lockett Home in St. Anne's Road, Marshside that took children into care whose parents were unable for whatever reasons to look after them. They also took in children for adoption. It was a voluntary Church of England Children's Society home but that branch has now closed down and there are new houses there. My job was teaching the students to be nursery nurses.

My next post was matron of the Marshside Residential Home for elderly people. It had sixty beds and came under the auspices of Southport Corporation's Social Service Dept.

About this time, Jean married Norman and gave birth to their son Paul so, for a while, she gave up work to look after her baby.

I went back to the Bradstock Lockett in 1974 when Paul was six months old, just helping out. They had a crèche so I could take him with me.

A few months later, I felt the hankering to go back to work again so I had a word with a friend who worked at the Promenade Hospital and asked them if there were any night duties going. I was asked to go for an interview and filled in a CV. Next thing, I got a call from Miss Barrett, the night sister and two weeks later I was offered a job, working Wednesday and Friday nights.

When the Prom closed in 1989, I moved to the new Southport & Formby General Hospital at Kew, later to become the Southport & Ormskirk General Hospital. I was on Ward 4a, acute medical. We had heart and stroke patients but no operations.

The difference was amazing from when I first started nursing. Although there was a higher level of staff, many of the rules we had been taught were now discarded. Nurses no longer wore their outside uniforms to keep the germs and dirt off their uniforms. The starched aprons were replaced by plastic ones and we wore paper caps (which were eventually discarded). I still wore my black tights and lace up shoes but it was no longer compulsory. Everyone now wore white dresses with green or blue belts. Sisters were in dark blue. Later, the uniform was changed again, this time to tunic tops and navy trousers.

Nurses no longer did any cleaning in the wards. 'Not my job', they would say. That was the province of the contract cleaners.

Some wards had mixed sexes in them, which caused distress and embarrassment for many patients, especially women.

All patients had televisions and phones by their bed but they had to pay for a card to activate them and they were charged an extortionate amount for phone calls. And they were charged each time they switched the TV on, not for how long they watched it so many of them kept it on all day as, if they switched off to wait for a later programme they would have to pay to switch it on again.

When I was in hospital for one night in 2004, I was appalled at the telephone charges. £5 to activate the card in the first place and 30p a minute for an INCOMING call! And no mobile phones allowed. Talk about robbing the sick. You wouldn't mind so much if all the money went to the hospital but the whole operation was run by a private firm.

As well as the Promenade Hospital shutting, most of the wards in the old Southport Infirmary in Scarisbrick New Road were transferred to the new hospital and now that building is three quarters empty apart from an ophthalmic section and the old Bob Martin's and Boothroyd Wards for Alzheimer's patients and people suffering from anxiety and depression.

I have now retired but I've never regretted leaving my village as I have found great satisfaction looking after the sick and I've been blessed with a loving husband and lovely grandson, Dominic.

I think it is Norman who is the lucky one. Having survived a stroke and a heart attack, he has his own personal nurse on hand to look after him. Jean's nursing days are not over.

MARCEL ZACHARIAH

Marcel was born in Egypt in December 1944. His family fled to Israel during the Suez crisis and came over to England in 1957, first to a refugee camp in Gloucester and then on to Southport where they settled in March 1958. Marcel's father, a qualified solicitor, got a job as a porter at the Scarisbrick Hotel.

Back in 1959, I was working in the Book Dept at W.H. Smiths, which was then situated at 479-481 Lord Street. When the paperboys failed to turn up, which seemed to happen most mornings, I was handed a red bicycle with the morning's newspapers stuffed into cloth panniers on the sides, and sent out in the rain or snow to deliver them.

One of those paperboys was a little Jewish lad with black curly hair and a big smile. This was Marcel Zachariah. From this inauspicious start he became one of Southport's leading property developers.

I couldn't speak English when I came to Southport, only Arabic and French. I was sent to Christ Church School and mastered the language by reading 'David Copperfield' in conjunction with an English dictionary.

Our family lived in two rented bedsits in Bank Square before moving to 35 Seabank Road. Later we bought the house and my mother opened a hairdressing salon in a back room. She had paid £60 for a six-month course at Alan's School of Hairdressing in West Street at the corner of Scarisbrick Avenue.

I worked part-time at W.H. Smiths delivering papers and at weekends I had a job at Pleasureland on The Fly shooting gallery. When I left school, I went as an apprentice to Andre Bernard's hairdressing salon in London Street and was with them for two and a half years before moving to their Ipswich and London branches. There were 25 branches in the country altogether.

I came back to Southport in 1962 and bought a shop in Compton Road where I set up my first hairdressing salon. I called it Marcel's and I was there for over five years.

On February 13th 1968, I opened up a second shop in Bold Street, also called Marcel's. It was a great success. We had a staff of fourteen including a manicurist, beautician, receptionist and seven apprentices. I loved hairdressing. It was sociable and fashionable and, if you were good, the tips paid for your lunch and a night out with a few drinks.

Our main competitors at the time were Andre Bernard's and John's in Lord Street, later bought by Tony Marriott who re-named it Headlines and went on to open a chain of shops.

Marcel's third acquisition was 79 London Street in 1971 when he sold Compton Road and teamed up with fellow hair stylist, Doug Edmondson, who was well-known as a guitarist with Southport's top group of the late 50's, The Teenbeats

I'd met Doug met Andre Bernard's where he was also an apprentice. Now he had his own salon, Michael Douglas, in Longton. Our first venture together was financing a deal for Dave Sperrin who sold sound equipment from his shop in Shakespeare Street. We put up £200 to buy six amplifiers for him to sell to local beat groups.

We called the salon at London Street, Bonnie's, and Peter Rose was in charge. Upstairs there were two flats and a bedsit that we rented out. It was our first venture as landlords and it prompted us to buy 89 London Street, which was dilapidated, but we converted it into three shops and four flats. We let the shops and sold the flats.

It was at that moment I asked myself, 'how many haircuts would I have to do to make that kind of turnover?' The answer was, two years of haircuts. I decided to go into property!

But Marcel was not content in being just a landlord; he wanted to build new houses and apartments.

In 1971-2, we built two semis in Fylde Road and 12 flats in Carr Lane. We just managed to complete them before the 3-day week came in and it took us two years to sell them. We lost money. Everybody got paid but we had to start again from square one. We decided that future projects would be in more upmarket areas and our next purchase was 2 Grosvenor Road.

Tragedy hit the family in 1973 when Marcel's brother, Isaac (Zak), died of medical problems following a car crash. After their bad experience at new-builds, Marcel and Doug turned their attention back to renting and built up a stock of flats and houses which were let to private and commercial tenants.

We owned about sixty units, all self-contained, in different parts of the town. The best thing to happen for private landlords was the Poll Tax because the tenants started paying the rates instead of the landlords, which meant an immediate rise in profits, and this followed on when Poll Tax was replaced by Council Tax.

Unfortunately, the quality of tenants in the private sector declined alarmingly over the years. People weren't taking care of the flats and, coupled with the problems caused by housing benefits and the delay in receiving the payments, we decided to dispose of all our residential properties.

In 1987, they decided to diversify into nursing homes.

Nursing homes were booming in the eighties. We bought 21 Argyle Road in 1987, a house in seven flats and we converted it into the Argyle Nursing Home with 24 beds. Next came Manchester House in Albert Road. The property had housed a charity home for the Jewish blind people. We turned it into a nursing home for 72 residents. We also acquired Argyle Park at 9 Park Road and Blair House at 18 Roe Lane. Blair House was another ex-blind home, the Godfrey Ermen Home, and we called it Blair House because we signed the contract on the day New Labour came to power.

We still own the nursing homes but government legislation has killed the whole thing off. So many homes have closed down and their owners gone bankrupt over the last decade. To give you an example, in 1987 our fees were £275 and we paid care assistants £2.20p an hour. Today (2006) the fees are £420 a week and care assistants get £5.50p an hour, on top of which the number of residents in each home has been reduced. We've lost 8 beds in Manchester House alone but we are lucky as most of our rooms are singles. It is difficult, too, finding reliable care workers. We use a lot of Fillipino girls. They're conscientious, caring and very religious.

Ninety per cent of our residents have their fees paid by Social Services and have to be assessed by them before they come in. We only take private patients if they can prove they will be able to pay the fees for the rest of their lives, simply because if they were to find themselves unable to pay at some point, social services would not pick up the tab.

We are only able to keep going because of our property interests. We could not make a living on the profits from the nursing homes alone.

Marcel's hairdressing salon in Bold Street is still going strong today but Marcel no longer works in it.

Hairdressing is for young people. We are concentrating these days on building. Our latest project is in Formby. Along with Mark Ellis, we have bought the old mushroom farm in Cable Street and are building 37 quality houses there that should be ready for occupation in 2007.

Marcel and Doug have also successfully renovated Highton's old furniture shop in Lord Street, turning it into the Royal Arcade with units let to various antique dealers. Doug no longer plays in The Teenbeats (or The Rocking Zimmers as they were later called!).

In 2002, Marcel, along with Councillor Barry Griffiths, decided to celebrate Southport's history of land speed racing (Sir Henry Seagrave and Sir Malcolm Campbell both attempted the world land speed record on Southport and Birkdale sands) by holding an historic motor show in Victoria Park. The following year, Sefton Council went into partnership with Marcel and the North West Historic Motor Show has become an annual event featuring vintage, veteran and classic cars, motor-cycles, commercial and military vehicles.

Certainly one can say that Marcel has made his mark on the town and, after such a difficult start, his story should be an inspiration to every paper boy riding a battered red carrier bike.

INDEX: People

INDEX: Subjects and Places